MW01196177

WHY IS IT
NAMED THAT?

**Stories Behind the Names
Of Over 300 Places
in Madison County and Huntsville, Alabama**

by Dex Nilsson

**Twinbrook Communications
Huntsville, Alabama**

WHY IS IT NAMED THAT?
Copyright 2003, 2005, 2018 by John Dexter Nilsson

TABLE OF CONTENTS

About This Book 4
About the Author 5
Acknowledgements 6

1. The Beginning of Madison County and Huntsville .. 7
2. County Cities and Communities 10
3. Roads in the County 20
4. Downtown Huntsville Streets 30
5. Streets in Huntsville's Five Points District 40
6. More Huntsville Streets 48
7. In and Around Madison 66
8. Buildings 71
9. Libraries 93
10. High Schools 96
11. Colleges and Universities 100
12. Mountains, Creeks, and Bridges 113
13. Parks and Recreation Areas 119
14. Redstone Arsenal 128
15. More Places of Interest 136

Bibliography 146
Index 151

The 2005 version of *Why Is It Named That?* is available in its entirety on the HuntsvilleHistoryCollection.org web site.

ABOUT THIS BOOK

Names of places, especially those named after people, fascinate me. This little book is the result of my curiosity. I published it in 2003, made some corrections in 2005, and have now expanded it (mostly in 2017) for this 2018 edition. There are over 60 new entries, and many previous write-ups have been improved.

History is all around us, much of it in the names of places we see every day. Befitting Alabama's bicentennial celebration of 2017-2019, included are name stories of the earliest Madison County settlers and the people who formed Huntsville before and after it was named. More names reflect county growth and city expansion, the era of the great cotton mills, establishment of Redstone Arsenal, and the arrival of German scientists who changed Huntsville from the Watercress Capitol of the World to Rocket City, U.S.A. Important too are many philanthropies that have made recent growth remarkable. All together, they form a 2018 photograph of Madison County, Madison, and Huntsville.

Within each chapter, names including first names are presented in alphabetical order. The book is uneven – for some entries I could find no more information than that presented. For others I had to condense a lot of information into a few paragraphs.

Much information came from libraries. Some came from county deed and will records. More was found in cemetery records. And from Internet files that seemed reliable. Still other material came from conversations with knowledgeable people. A lot came from my driving around, checking signs and names of places.

As I wrote above, there is history in the names we see every day. May you discover that history – and enjoy *Why Is It Named That?*

ABOUT THE AUTHOR

Dex Nilsson was born in Washington, D.C., in 1930. He grew up in Indiana, attended Phillips Academy at Andover, and obtained a B.S. degree from Purdue University. In 1954 he arrived in Huntsville to accept a job with Thiokol Chemical Corporation.

Dex joined the Huntsville Little Theatre, which Nancy Mitchell had founded five years earlier. They were in a play together and within a year were married. They acted and directed and both served terms as president. Dex helped form Huntsville's Arts Council - he was its first Treasurer - and is credited in helping create the Von Braun Center.

In 1962 Dex moved across Redstone Arsenal to join General Electric Company. In 1966 when GE lost its contract to support NASA's Computation Laboratory, he and his family moved to Maryland where he managed the writing/publishing activities of GE's computer services organization. He and Nancy continued acting/directing with theatre groups in the nearby Washington, D.C., area, and Dex was a leader in the arts of Rockville and Montgomery County, MD. Nancy became a successful regional playwright. In 2001 they returned to Huntsville.

In addition to this book, Dex wrote and published *Discover Why It's Named That ...*, how 190 places on the Maryland Eastern Shore got their names. He followed with *The Names of Washington, D.C.*, containing 275 stories about places in the capital city, first time such information had been compiled. He edited and published *The Story of the First Airborne Battalion* by Harris Mitchell, the battalion's sergeant major and Huntsville's civil defense director during the Cold War years. He published some of Nancy's plays in *All I Could See – and Seven More Plays*. In 2016 he published his own life story, *Autobiography of a Book Man*. The older books sometimes show up on eBay; his autobiography is currently available through Amazon.com.

ACKNOWLEDGEMENTS

My 2003 edition contained a solid page and a half of names that I acknowledged helped me put that original book together. Most of those people have now moved on, which is the main reason I have not relisted them here. Instead here are some of the people who have helped with the new entries to this edition:

Jim Batson for update on the Blake family and Blake Bottom Road.
Deane Dayton for reference to Michael Ward's book about the UAH Foundation and the story behind Thornton Research Park.
Winter Forest for a quick tour and Huntsville Depot information.
Reagan Grimsley, university archivist at UAH, for information about Morton, Salmon, Wilson, and other campus names.
Faye Grimwood about her family and Grimwood Road.
Kathy Guido, Delaware designer, for this book's covers.
Katelyn Henderson, Botanical Garden marketing manager, for a lot of BG information.
Nancy Wells Hofues for the story of Wells Road in Meridianville.
Steve Ivy, Huntsville Parks and Recreation director and his management staff for information about park places and names.
John Mayes for the origin of Stoner Park.
David Robb for the story of the early Mississippi Territory and Levi Lincoln.
David J. Slyman, Jr., for his email about the name Providence.
Odalys Miranda Suastegui, archives assistant at Oakwood University, for information regarding Oakwood names.
Cassandra Thompson, archivist at the Huntsville-Madison County Library, for information about Jane Grote Roberts.
Eunice Tibbs for family information regarding Dan Tibbs Road.
Brian Walker, Huntsville landscape department manager, for an update on Wellman Family Park.

1. THE BEGINNING OF MADISON COUNTY AND HUNTSVILLE

ALABAMA. First, a few words about the word *Alabama*. In short, its meaning is not known.

A southern Creek Indian tribe lived in what is now central Alabama. The area's major river was named *Alabama* for this tribe. The state name in turn came from the name of the river.

The name appears in several spellings in the logs of early European explorers, the first being in the accounts of the Hernando de Soto expedition of 1540. But some believe that the writers referred to a tribe of Chickasaw Indians, not the tribe mentioned above. Some investigators believe the word comes from the Choctaw Indians. Words in that language that approximate *Alabama* translate to "thicket clearers." It is also popular belief that the word stands for "here we rest." That derivation came from writers in the 1840s and 1850s. But experts searching the Muskogean language used by the Creeks, Chickasaws, and Choctaws have been unable to find any word or phrase that could translate with that meaning. All this according to the Alabama Department of Archives and History in Montgomery.

What is left of the Alabama tribe can today be found in the Big Thicket part of Texas east of Livingston where it shares its reservation with the Coushatta tribe. You can visit and enjoy camping, swimming, and fishing in Lake Tombigbee.

MADISON COUNTY. Georgia originally claimed all lands from the Atlantic Ocean to the Mississippi River, and after it became a state and set its western border, it still claimed those lands. In 1802, President Jefferson sent a commission to negotiate buying the lands in the northern part of the area. The commission was made up of James Madison, secretary of state, Albert Gallatin, secretary of the treasury, and Levi Lincoln, attorney general. Purchase was successful, and the northern portion of the Mississippi Territory came into being. The land was still occupied by Indians, but in 1805 the Chickasaw and Cherokee Indians began ceding their lands to the U.S. government. Even before that time, trappers, traders, and settlers had begun to move into the area. In December 1808, only a few days after Madison had been elected the next president, Territorial governor Robert Williams created Madison County and named it in honor of the new president.

President Madison immediately ordered a census taken. The area was surveyed and laid out into sections. In 1809 settlers could claim their lands and purchase them from the government for a small fee – as low as $2 an acre – with credit available. By the end of 1809, 24,000 acres had been bought and registered through the federal land office in Nashville. Land prices began to rise.

The city of Huntsville was formally laid out in 1810.

After Mississippi became a state in March 1817, an act of Congress organized the remaining land as the Alabama Territory. A constitutional convention met in Huntsville in 1819. On December 14 of that year Congress passed a resolution that admitted Alabama into the Union, and President Monroe signed it into law. Huntsville became the first capital of Alabama.

HUNTSVILLE. The City is named for its first settler, John Hunt. Hunt's family was Scotch-Irish and had settled in Pennsylvania, later in Virginia. John Hunt served in the Revolutionary War as a private. In the 1780s, the family was in North Carolina where Hunt was the first sheriff of Hawkins

County. By the 1790s, he was in Tennessee and he was sheriff of Claiborne County. In 1804 Hunt saw the great limestone spring Indians had talked about and a year later brought his family to settle here. He completed a two-room cabin and established the community that would later bear his name.

The city of Huntsville was created in 1810. The original plat consisted of 20 blocks, laid out in a 4 by 5 grid. The resulting streets were named for the heroes of the time.

In 1866 the town expanded to four square miles. It wasn't until 1925 that the town took East Huntsville into its city limits. With the advent of its rocket and missile business in the 1950s, the population exploded from 16,000 to over 72,000, then in the 1960s to almost 140,000. Today, population is over 191,000, the city has spread over 214 square miles, and it is the third largest city in the state behind only Birmingham and Montgomery.

If he could return, I wonder what John Hunt would say.

2. COUNTY CITIES AND COMMUNITIES

There are six incorporated cities in Madison County: Gurley, Huntsville, Madison, New Hope, Owens Cross Roads, and Triana. And there are many communities, some of which are larger than some of the incorporated cities. Some are so small that you can drive through them and not know you were there. Here are over two dozen that have intriguing names.

BELL FACTORY. One of the first communities of the county in which people settled was Three Forks of Flint, on the Flint River, and in the area now known as Riverton. Downstream of where the forks came together was a grain mill. Horatio Jones bought the grain mill, and he and subsequent leaders turned the site into the Bell Factory. The factory made yarn, and starting in 1832, it manufactured cotton cloth so successfully that it was known as the "Early Pride of Huntsville." The original mill began in 1819, burned down in 1841, was replaced with new buildings, and operated until 1885.

Water on the river was forced over a wheel or turbine, which gave power to the factory. Since no steam was involved, the factory had no whistle. Instead a bell was rung. Hence the name.

BOBO. Arvin J. Bobo served in the Virginia Cavalry during the Civil War - but not on the side most Southerners might think when they read that. He was from Ohio, and when that state stopped recruiting soldiers, he went across the river to West Virginia, which was then part of Virginia, to join the Union army. Many Ohioans fought in this area, and some returned after the war. Arvin did so in 1888, with his wife Margaret and large family. They came by riverboat from Charleston, West Virginia, to Louisville, then by train to Athens, along with all their family goods and farm animals. Once in Athens, they assembled their wagons and made their way to "the barrens" of Madison County, where Arvin had purchased land. The family farmed and prospered, and the community in the northwest part of the county became known as Bobo. Arvin and Margaret are buried in the Golightly Cemetery just off Bobo Section Road.

BUCKHORN. As early as 1808, a tavern here provided a stop for people traveling from Winchester, Tennessee, to Madison County, on what is now Winchester Road. Supposedly the tavern got the name Buckhorn in 1858 when William L. Fanning killed a buck near the site and presented its antlers to the tavern.

CHASE. A post office was established here in 1889 with the name Mercury, from the Roman messenger of the gods. In 1908, the name was changed to Chase, for the family that had established nurseries here a few years earlier.

From 1889 to 1906, the Chase brothers developed their nursery knowledge by studying with their cousins in Rochester, New York, where the cousins operated nationally known New England Nurseries. The cousins provided the capital, and the Chase family - Herbert, Charles, Robert, and Henry - came to the Huntsville area because of its wonderful soil. Theirs was no small nursery start-up either: Elizabeth Chapman wrote "They planted seventy-five acres in three hundred thousand apple trees and the rest in pears, cherries, and plums." They organized in the Normal area in 1906 as Chase Nurseries, with Henry B. Chase as president. Henry, who had his home on Adams Street in Huntsville, also served as head of the city council from 1916 to 1918, then defeated W. T. Hutchens by three votes to become mayor from 1918 to 1920.

CLUTTSVILLE. A "map in the files of G.W. Jones & Sons ... drawn about 1850" shows the Clutts settlement in the northwest part of the county - apparently one of the earliest in the county. There is a record of sale of land in the area by Davy Clutts in

1868, and subsequent transactions by other family members throughout the late 1800s.

DAN. This tiny community is just about at the junction of Shady Grove Road and Wall-Triana Highway. It is named for Dan Turner. The Turner family here dates from the early 1800s. Rev. H.P. Turner was the first preacher - back in those days a circuit rider - assigned to the Shady Grove United Methodist Church. Dan had its own post office from 1878 to 1901.

DEPOSIT. In 1812 the Creek Indians became troublesome, and Andrew Jackson organized an army of volunteers, the Tennessee Militia, to fight. In 1813 he built a fort where Thompson's Creek ran into the Tennessee River in Marshall County. It was used to deposit and store supplies as the militia moved on. The road used by Jackson's troops from New Market to Fort Deposit was called Deposit Road, and ran through this point, just southeast of Buckhorn. A post office, now discontinued, was established here in 1888 with the name Deposit.

DITTO LANDING. James (or John) Ditto might have been the first settler in Madison County, arriving from North Carolina in 1802, about two years before John Hunt. He set up an Indian trading post near Chickasaw Island (which was later renamed Hobbs Island) on the Tennessee River. In 1807 he built a ferry and carried passengers across the river. That effort expanded into a shipyard, and Ditto's boats traversed the river all the way through the shoals. About 1820, James Hardie operated a store at Ditto's Landing. It was a busy port: Hardie wrote, "From this place all the cotton made [in Madison County] is shipped to New Orleans . . . about 15,000 to 17,000 bales. . . ."

Today Ditto Landing Park is site of camp sites, a marina, docks, boat ramps, and pavilions. It is at the Tennessee River just east of Whitesburg Drive on Hobbs Island Road. Its main entrance road is marked for W. Eugene Morgan, one of the original Marina and Port Authority board members in the 1970s.

ELON. This tiny community on Hobbs Island Road just west of New Hope has only a church sign to identify it. Elon is Hebrew for oak.

FANNINGS CROSSING. This spot a mile or so north of Buckhorn is probably named for the same Fanning family as the hunter at Buckhorn. Winchester Road crossed a branch of the Flint River at this point.

FARLEY. John Benton Farley was born in 1860 near what was then Whitesburg. He married Mattie Elizabeth McGaha in 1882. He became a doctor and practiced medicine. They had three children. This area now within Huntsville, near the intersection of Whitesburg Drive and Green Cove Road, is said to take its name from Dr. Farley. There is no sign marking the area except for Farley Elementary School.

In her book on place name origins, Virginia Foscue attributes the name to Dr. Farley's appointment as the first postmaster, in 1893. But in a typed history in the Huntsville Public Library, Ruth Ross claims an 1818 map shows a place called Farley that encompassed over 2,000 acres - indication that Dr. Farley's parents must have been among the area's first settlers.

FISK. The community known as Fisk grew up where the West Fork of the Flint River crosses U.S. 231/431 a couple miles north of Hazel Green. Several Fisks are shown in the 1850 census, oldest of whom is Goodwin, a farmer from South Carolina. A post office was established in 1885. John and Will Fisk had a house and store about 1908 or 1910, and a Cabe Fisk ran a steam powered gin in the area. In 1929 a flood destroyed the village. A small road named Flood Lane commemorated that event, but the road was renamed Floyd Harbin Lane in 2015.

13

2. County Cities and Communities

GURLEY. The Memphis and Charleston Railway reached here in 1857, and the community was called Gurley's Tank (because a steam train's engine took on water here) and later Gurleyville. Its post office was established in 1866, but the name was shortened to Gurley in 1883. The town was incorporated in 1891.

Captain Frank B. Gurley obtained notoriety when he commanded a local cavalry unit under General Nathan Bedford Forrest during the Civil War. But this town's name comes from his father, John Gurley, one of the county's pioneers.

HAMPTON COVE. The building development that became the Hampton Cove community was begun by the Hays family. James Hays told me that the family of his mother, Annie Wade Street Hays, was descended from Wade Hampton III, the Confederate general and South Carolina senator. Thus Hampton Cove got its name from that Hays family name.

Wade Hampton II was a colonel on Andrew Jackson's staff at the Battle of New Orleans during the War of 1812. James Record has written that in 1810, Hampton arranged for construction of Fort Hampton on the Elk River in neighboring Limestone County.

Wade Hampton III was born in Charleston in 1818, graduated from the University of South Carolina, studied law but never practiced, became a planter, and served in the state house of representatives (1852-1856) and senate (1858-1861). He commanded Hampton's Legion in the Confederate Army during the Civil War and by 1865 was a lieutenant general. He became Governor of South Carolina in 1876, and rose to the U.S. Senate in 1878 where he served until 1891. He died in 1902.

HARBINVILLE. Thomas Nathan Harbin was born in 1904, a son of James Enoch Harbin, Jr., and Odie Lee Wolaver. Tom farmed, then for 35 years operated a general store, later Harbin

Grocery, at the corner of Greenville Pike and Joe Quick Road. That's where the small community there takes its name. Tom died in 1978.

HARVEST. This community's name was originally Kelly, after Thomas B. Kelly, who was postmaster in 1905. The Kelly family had orchards, and from among their crops, shipped "Early Harvest Apples." Several growers along Ford Chapel Road did the same. The current name comes from those apples. (See Jeff.)

HAZEL GREEN. There were early settlers reported in the area between 1804 and 1809. The post office was established in 1829. Several sources say that the community takes its name from the green hazelnut trees in the area. But Frankie Glynn, writing in *The Huntsville Times* of January 28, 1968, says that Robert Irwin was its first store owner in 1809 and its first postmaster, and that Hazel Green is named after his wife, Hazel.

HOBBS ISLAND. Hubbard Hobbs was a Revolutionary War soldier. He and his wife Martha raised a large family. Hubbard died in 1817, and Martha moved to Alabama in 1820. Her oldest son, John, had settled in Madison County where he traded with the Indians, and owned a lot of land, including the island in the Tennessee River and the nearby community that still bear his name.

JEFF. Joshua O. Kelly bought land here in 1853. His father is said to have come, with others of his family, to Madison County from Virginia in 1819 and to have settled off what is now Pulaski Pike. There have been Kelly descendants in the area ever since. With his two sons, David E. and Joshua, Jr., Joshua formed successful mercantile, blacksmith, ginning, and farming businesses. The sons eventually applied for a post office to be named Jeff Davis in honor of the president of the Confederacy. They were told the name had to be one word only, so settled on

15

Jeff. Today at Jeff is Kelly Drive, and just to its south, Kelly Springs Road.

A different story: Jesse Richardson in his *Alabama Encyclopedia* writes that, much earlier than the above, there was a Cherokee Indian settlement at the headwaters of Indian Creek, and when white settlers arrived, the name Jeffs Village had already been given to the settlement "because the head man bore that name."

LICK SKILLET. At the corner of Charity Lane and Butter and Egg Road, the place has been known as Lick Skillet since the 1920s. Bill Malone, a disc jockey from Fayetteville, Tennessee, says his grandfather had a general store there. He got in a fight, grabbed a skillet, and used it for a blow to the head, ending the fight. Maybe that's where the name came from.

MADISON. Aside from Huntsville, this is the largest city in the county. According to the official Madison web site, the city covers 23 square miles. Population as of 2015 was estimated at 47,000. (See 7. In and Around Madison.)

MAYSVILLE. May was probably the name of the local family who settled in the area about 1838. A post office was established in 1850. Maysville appears in the 1890 census with a population of 218. That was the only time it appeared on the census rolls.

MERIDIANVILLE. It is directly on and takes its name from the Madison County survey line made in 1809. The community first appeared in the U.S. census of 1880, but then did not appear again for a century.

MONROVIA. It seems unlikely that it is named for a local Monroe or President Monroe, and it does not appear on the 1850 county map. It might have been named after the Civil War by freed slaves for the capital city of Liberia where Monrovia is the major city of over a million people. Some people have suggested it was simply named by a settler (unknown) from Monrovia, Indiana. Jim Forte's *Postal History* says a post office operated as Monrovia, AL, from 1878 to 1904.

MOONTOWN. Unlike Huntsville, it doesn't have anything to do with space or the moon. This small community of farms just east of Huntsville takes its name from the Moon family. In 1814 Richard Moon patented land in this part of the county. Also in the county, in 1820, John and Hester Moon were married. John had come from Pennsylvania. In 1826 they had a daughter, Mary Ann "Polly" Moon. In 1842, she married Andrew Sublett. Today, the Moontown area is home to many Moon and Sublett descendants.

MOORES MILL. This rapidly expanding community takes its name from the mill that once stood to its north on the Flint River. (See 3. Moores Mill Road.)

NEBO. A community, road, and mountain several miles east of New Hope have this name. Nebo is a biblical name - according to Deuteronomy 34, Moses died on Mount Nebo.

NEW HOPE. The first settler was William Cloud, and in the 1820s the community was called Cloud's Town. In 1832, the community tried to organize with the name Vienna, but there already was a Vienna in Alabama (down on the Tombigbee River). So the community grew up using the name from its Methodist Church. In 1834 the New Hope post office was officially established, and in 1956 the town was incorporated.

NEW MARKET. In 1804 Isaac and Joseph Criner settled near here on the Mountain Fork of the Flint River, becoming the earliest settlers in this part of the county. The first settlement in New Market itself was made in 1806. A post office was officially established in 1836. Idea behind the place name was to establish "a new market" for farmers of the area.

New Market is one of the most common community names in the United States. The oldest Newmarket in the country is the one in New Hampshire, named in 1727 for Newmarket in County Suffolk, England.

OWENS CROSSROADS. This community was named for its first postmaster, Thomas P. Owens, appointed in 1869. The city was incorporated in 1967.

PLEVNA. Hickory Flat was the first name of this community, from its many hickory trees and flat land. A post office was opened in 1878. In 1886, the railroad arrived, running south all the way to Hobbs Island, and the name of the community was changed to Plevna. Railroad conductor Lev Jones is credited with choosing the name, but why he selected it isn't recorded. The name reportedly comes from a city in Russia, the location of a fortress during the Russo-Turkish War of 1877. There are also Plevnas in Missouri, Kansas, and Montana.

PROVIDENCE. Although part of Huntsville, this community likes to view itself as a separate village. It was begun by David Slyman, Jr., who wrote "after much research and over 2,000 names, we chose Providence because of the similarities in the, architecture, being on water, and its sense of place" – compared to Providence, Rhode Island.

RYLAND. Russel J. Kelly owned land here, and the village was named Kelly's Crossing, because one had to cross Kelly's land to get to it. When Kelly died, Virgil Homer Ryland bought some of the land and established a general store and post office. Virgil was the first postmaster, appointed in 1895, so the community took its name from him. He served as postmaster until 1898. He died in 1900.

SWANCOTT. The "cott" suffix comes from the Old English "cot" and indicates, among other meanings, a place of shelter.

There is a Swan Pond nearby in the Wheeler National Wildlife Refuge and a Swan Creek close in Limestone County. And, yes, there are swans in the area.

TONEY. Virginia Foscue attributes the name to Blanche R. Toney, the first postmaster, appointed in 1898, but Toneys were in the area much earlier. There's a marriage record of Elijah Toney, Jr., in 1856, and it's known that he and his family lived on nearby Shady Grove Road. In an undated typed manuscript in the Heritage Room of the library, Edna McClure of Toney has written that the first postmaster was Blanche, but the settlement was named for a Jim Toney.

TRIANA. Much early area transportation was along rivers. Triana became an important port where Indian Creek flowed into the Tennessee River. The village was incorporated in 1819, and a post office was established in 1821.

In 1821 Huntsvillians Thomas Fearn and the wealthy LeRoy Pope headed the Indian Creek Navigation Company to build a canal to connect Hunt's spring to the Tennessee River at Triana via Indian Creek. It was used to ship cotton as early as 1827, and it was completed in 1835. But within ten years, Whitesburg Pike became a faster route from Huntsville to the Tennessee, and Triana's days as a major port began to ebb.

The name Triana is said to be taken from that of a sailor who came to the New World with Columbus. Who picked it or why isn't known. Indeed, there was a Juan Verde de Triana on the Pinta and a Fernando de Triana on the Nina.

3. ROADS IN THE COUNTY

ALBERT HALL HIGHWAY. The portion of U.S. 72 from Gurley to Shields Road has been named for state representative Albert Hall. He served District 22 in the Alabama legislature from 1978 until his death in 2006, just after being re-elected to his eighth term. A sign giving his name is at mile marker 112.

ARDMORE HIGHWAY. In 1873, the Pennsylvania Railroad changed the name of its Athensville. PA, station to Ardmore. The name was chosen by the many Irish immigrants in the area. Ardmore is a Gaelic word signifying high ground or hills.

Northwest of Huntsville Jordan Lane becomes Highway 53 which joins Huntsville and Ardmore, Alabama. The town was originally named Austin, for Alex Austin, who selected the name for a station on the Louisville & Nashville Railroad. However, in 1922 the railroad changed the name to Ardmore, reportedly for the name-changed community in Pennsylvania.

BLAKE BOTTOM ROAD. It runs west-east from Nance Road north of Madison across Research Park Boulevard and across the Ardmore Highway into northwest Huntsville. The Hall, Wade, and Blake families have owned lands in the area of the road going back to the early 1800s – and they still do. (For more about the Blakes, see 12. B.W. Blake Bridge.)

BOB WADE LANE. Littleberry and David Wade came from Virginia to Madison County in 1817, Littleberry settling in the Big Cove area and David on what is now Bob Wade Lane. David turned his land into a large cotton plantation, and his initial cabin into a fine home. David and his wife, Eliza Grantland, had six children, one of whom was Robert B. Wade. Robert moved to his own land near Big Cove, so when David died in the early

1860s, the plantation was left to two single daughters, Amanda and Harriet. They ran the plantation successfully until their deaths in the 1890s. At that time, the land was left to Robert's son, also named Robert B. Wade. There once was a Wade Cemetery, but with no markers and no record of who was buried there. In 1940, the final Robert B. Wade was buried in Maple Hill Cemetery.

BROWNS FERRY ROAD. This road stretches from Madison through parts of Huntsville across Limestone County and eventually to Browns Ferry Nuclear Plant on the Tennessee River about ten miles southwest of Athens. In the mid-1800s there was a Brown's ferry operating here for people needing to cross the river. Started in 1973, the nuclear plant is TVA's first and largest with three boiling water reactors. It sits on 840 acres, has 1,400 on-site employees, and can generate enough power to serve two million homes.

CAPSHAW ROAD runs east-west from the community of Capshaw in neighboring Limestone County. Virginia Foscoe attributes the name to Chickasaw words "bok kapassa" (meaning cold creek) or "oka kapassa" (cold water). However, James Record lists Capshaw as a community shown on an 1892 map, and adds the note "named after David Capshaw." John Rankin lists David and a William Capshaw as original land buyers in western Madison County or eastern Limestone County - the latter and its borders hadn't been established at the time.

COUNTESS ROAD. No royalty is involved, although the Countiss family obtained their first lands in America through a grant from Lord Calvert of Maryland. Eventually part of the family came to Alabama and settled in Tuscaloosa. There Ira Jackson Countiss was born in 1825. He married Nancy Margaret Durrett in 1848. One of their daughters, Stella, married a Methodist minister, W. James Reid. Reid was sent to Madison County to preach and sent back such glowing reports of the land that, by 1896, Ira and most of his children and families all moved here and located north of Huntsville. It was apparently Ira who changed the family name from Countiss to Countess.

There is an 1896 deed from Robert. B. Wade to Ira J. Countess for 80 acres. Bob Wade Lane is on the west side of U.S. 231, and Countess Road is the same road on the east side of U.S. 231, both just north of Huntsville.

DAN TIBBS ROAD. Big signs on Research Park Boulevard and Pulaski Pike mark their intersections with Dan Tibbs Road, an ordinary street that runs between the two. The first Daniel Tibbs arrived in the Huntsville area in 1863 and eventually owned lands north of Huntsville and around Harvest. He and his descendants were successful farmers. The name of the road is attributed to Dan Tibbs, Sr., who died in 1965 at age 75. The Tibbs family still owns land in the area.

DUG HILL ROAD. The road runs from north of Hampton Cove to U.S. 72 just west of Gurley. I could find no one by that name. Eleven Eastern states plus Ontario have a Dug Hill Road. Why the name is so popular isn't clear. Locally, perhaps someone brought the name to this area from Eastern Tennessee.

Union headquarters in Nashville ordered the 5th Tennessee Cavalry under Col. William Stokes to move to Sparta to rid the area of enemy guerrillas. Confederate Col. John Hughs of the 25th Tennessee Infantry Regiment had organized such rebel groups. In 1864 when the two groups clashed in the Tennessee woods, the Union cavalry forces were simply ambushed. They lost 40 men, the Confederates none. It is called the Battle of Dug Hill and is considered a minor skirmish of the Civil War.

FLOYD HARDIN LANE. Hardin was a popular barber from Huntsville's Five Points area. Following his death in 2014, Flood Lane, just north of Hazel Green, was re-named for him. He was a self-proclaimed "Mayor of Five Points" and was known for his help to those in need.

FORD'S CHAPEL ROAD. This road runs east-west between Wall-Triana Highway and Jeff Road. In 1810, Richard Ford bought land here. The first Methodist Society in the local circuit (preachers then were circuit riders) was organized at his home. He also allowed four acres of his land to be used as a campground for the Methodists, and by 1819 a church was set up. Richard and his wife Betsy eventually deeded the land and church to the Ford Chapel trustees so that it became Methodist property. The resulting Methodist church has undergone many renovations, but its sanctuary stands on its original foundation.

GRIMWOOD ROAD. In 1899, six Grimwood brothers moved from Kankakee County, Illinois, to Madison County. All six bought 80-acre plots in the north central part of the county. According to James Record, Rolland and Glen Grimwood grew the first lespedeza (a bush clover used for forage and soil improvement) in the county in 1911-12.

One of the first roads in the county extended west from the Hazel Green area to Brier Fork of the Flint River, then from that spot further west. In 1922, Rolland Grimwood filled in the spot and used logs to provide the necessary bridge. It was known as Grimwood Bridge, and it was soon after that that the entire road became known as Grimwood Road.

HEROES HIGHWAY. State representative Mac McCutcheon (R-Capshaw) has had U.S. Highways 231/431 officially designated Heroes Highway to honor the county's fallen law enforcement officers and firefighters. Green memorial signs are placed at intervals between Bob Wade Lane and the Tennessee State line. On a drive in 2017, signs honoring five men were sighted, for Deputy Sheriffs Thomas R. Lewis, Haskel G.

McLane, and Billy Joe Thrower, and for Officers Eric Freeman and Daniel Golden.

JIM WHITAKER HIGHWAY. Close to mile marker 318, south of Owens Cross Roads, on U.S. 431, there's a state-erected green sign naming the road the "Jim Whitaker Highway." It's named for the asphalt businessman who headed Whitaker Contracting Corporation in Guntersville, whose company paved the highway - and many other highways in northern Alabama.

JOE QUICK ROAD. This is the main road going east from the middle of Hazel Green and U.S. 231.

William Lafayette Quick was from Hardin County, Tennessee, where his father was a blacksmith. Will married Lucy Ann Maroney in 1882, and around 1900, they moved to Alabama, where he built a grist mill, cotton gin, sawmill, blacksmith forge and foundry, and had the first electric generator in the county.

Will also designed and built the first "flying machine" in Alabama (although it reportedly didn't fly too well). Will and Lucy eventually had ten children, eight of whom became early aviationists. Cady was one of the first women pilots, three sons were barnstormers, Curtis obtained a patent for his airplane crop duster, and Tom was a test pilot and another patent holder for his airplane emission control. Will died in 1927. He was inducted into the Alabama Hall of Fame in 1982, and his flying machine has been placed in the U.S. Space and Rocket Center.

Joe, another son, stayed on the ground. He was Madison County commissioner of District 1 for 24 years, from 1936 to 1960, and the road bears his name. When he took office, his district had no hard-surfaced roads. When he left, it had 150 miles of the best hard-surfaced roads in the region.

MARTIN LUTHER KING, JR., HIGHWAY. The highway north of Wade Mountain, between Research Boulevard and Pulaski Pike has been named for civil rights leader Dr. King.

In 1954, King was pastor of the Dexter Avenue Baptist Church in Montgomery. He hadn't been there a year when Rosa Parks defied segregated seating on a city bus. With Ralph Abernathy King organized a year-long boycott of city busing that made him known nationally as a civil rights leader. In 1960 he was pastor of the Ebenezer Baptist Church in Atlanta and president of the Southern Christian Leadership Conference (SCLC). In 1963 he organized a march on Washington and gave his "I have a dream" speech at the Lincoln Memorial. In 1964 he was the youngest recipient of the Nobel Peace Prize. A year later, following a voter registration campaign in Selma, King led an anti-segregation march from Selma to Montgomery.

King then shifted SCLC strategy to focus on economic issues. In 1967 he was planning another Washington march to demand an anti-poverty "economic bill of rights." He stopped during planning to assist striking sanitation workers in Memphis, where he was shot and killed.

MOORES MILL ROAD. Sam Darwin III has the farm to the north of where Moore's Mill stood. He remembers the mill from the 1930s. It ground corn and made meal. It stood on the north bank of the Flint River, just west of where the road crossed. The road was then called Hillsboro Road, and today's Moores Mill Road's bridge crossing isn't quite in the same place. Although his great grandmother married a Moore, we were unable to determine exactly which Moore lent his name to the mill.

All I could determine from courthouse files was that, in the 1820s, Benjamin, David, Gabriel, James, John, and William Moore all bought land in Madison County. The Moores closest to the mill location were John and Emily, who bought land there

25

3. Roads in the County

from William Blankenship in 1871.

NICK DAVIS ROAD. This road runs west from Jeff Road all the way to Athens in Limestone County. Virginian Nicholas Davis was one of neighboring Limestone County's earliest settlers. He was a delegate to the Alabama constitution convention in Huntsville in 1819, later was state senator, even ran for governor. He and his wife, Martha Hargrave, had a son Nick Davis, Jr., born in Limestone County.

In 1852, after serving during the Mexican War, Nick, Jr., became a lawyer with his practice in Huntsville. He served two terms in the state legislature, was a lieutenant colonel of the Alabama Infantry during the Civil War (but didn't see action), and after the war returned to his law practice. His wife was Sophia Lowe, daughter of Bartley M. Lowe. (See 4. Lowe Avenue.) Nick Davis, Jr., died in 1874.

OLD RAILROAD BED ROAD cuts across the northwest portion of the county, running through Harvest, Toney, Bobo, and Elkwood, and yes, it follows an old railroad bed - that of the Nashville, Chattanooga, and St. Louis Railroad (the N.C.&L), which operated from 1887 to 1929.

OPP REYNOLDS ROAD. This is an east-west road just south of Ready Section Road, in the northwest part of the county. The earliest Reynolds in the area for whom I could find a record was James W. Reynolds. He bought land in the area in 1858. He and his wife Elizabeth were from Kentucky. But later there really was a person with the odd name of Opp. Opp James Reynolds, from whom the road obviously takes its name, had land transactions in the area recorded at the courthouse in 1913 and 1917. He and his wife Minnie B. are buried in the Madison Cross Roads Cemetery. Opp's dates are 1881-1961.

3. Roads in the County

PAUL LUTHER BOLDEN MEMORIAL HIGHWAY. Bolden was the most decorated soldier from Madison County in World War II. In 2013, the 18-mile stretch of State Highway 53 was named in his honor. He lived on a farm near Ardmore and traveled that portion of the highway daily.

In Belgium in 1944, Sergeant Bolden's company was in an assault on a German house used as a strong point, but was pinned down by small arms fire. Bolden and a comrade charged through the fire, and Bolden threw in grenades, then entered the house, surprising 35 Nazi SS troops. With his submachine gun, Bolden killed 20 before he was hit - in the shoulder, chest, and stomach. He left the house to find his comrade killed, then waited outside for the Nazis to surrender. When none came out, he re-entered and shot the remaining 15, thus insuring the success of his company's mission. President Truman awarded Bolden the Medal of Honor, the nation's highest military honor. He was also a recipient of a Silver Star, four Bronze Stars, two Purple Hearts, and Belgian Croix de Guerre with Palm. He was one of the most decorated soldiers of the war.

Bolden was born at Hobbs Island. After the war, Bolden worked at Redstone Arsenal and lived on the farm near Ardmore. He and his wife Violet raised four sons and three daughters. Bolden died in 1979.

Huntsville also honored Bolden, naming the building housing the U.S. Veterans Memorial Museum for him.

READY SECTION ROAD is a major east-west road in the northwest corner of the county. Which Ready gave the road its name is unclear to me. Nicholas Ready bought land just west of Huntsville in 1820. But Elvin (Almo), Charles, John, and Jasper Ready (sometimes also spelled Reedy and Reddy) later bought land, apparently entire sections, all in the far northwest corner and in the vicinity of today's Ready Section Road. Some of these

Readys are buried in Ready Cemetery, which is two miles north of Toney; others are in Charity Cemetery, two miles northwest of Hazel Green.

In the Doolings' book, *Huntsville - A Picture History*, there's a picture of one-room Ready School. It was located about a mile south of Charity Church, just about at the eastern end of what is now Ready Section Road.

STEGER ROAD. In 1806, Francis Eppes Harris and his wife Mary Macon Harris moved from Virginia to Madison County, building a home about four miles from Huntsville. John Perratt Steger, Jr., also of Virginia, married the Harris daughter, Rebecca, and they too moved to Madison County, in 1810. They had nine children. One of them, just as an example, Kennon Harris Steger, became a successful farmer, married in 1838, and produced eleven children. Most of the Stegers located in the eastern portion of the county, and it isn't clear for which one, if indeed any single one, this road north of Huntsville is named.

Steger's Store stood on the west side of where Steger Road joins U.S. 231. A gin mill, grist mill, and blacksmith shop operated there from 1913 to 1952.

WALL-TRIANA HIGHWAY. This road runs north from Triana all the way to the Tennessee state line. Arthur Wall's grand nieces Jean Wall Lemley and Rebecca Wall have written that the north portion of the road was named for Arthur L. Wall, county commissioner of District 4 when the road was built. They found minutes of commission meetings, one of which is for September 5, 1927, that states "Paid H.C. Turner $175.80 for work on "Wall Highway" - first time that term appears.

WELLS ROAD. At the traffic light in Meridianville, the road that goes west is named Wells Road. I talked to a member of the Wells family who owns land on the road to see what Wells it was named for. Surprise: No Wells family member at all. The Wells name was given to the road well (pardon the pun) before the Civil War for a trio of wells in the area that were believed to have healthful waters.

WILLIS VON MOORE HIGHWAY. What many of us know as Research Park Boulevard is also Alabama Highway 255, and it has this name as a memorial to State Trooper Moore. In 1996 Moore responded to an emergency when his car was forced into a guard rail by several cars that refused to grant him right of way, the rail pierced his car, and he was killed. Moore was 34 years old and had been a trooper for only a year.

WINCHESTER ROAD. One of the earliest roads, it was used by settlers who arrived in Madison County from Tennessee. It then connected Winchester, Tennessee, with Madison County and Huntsville - and still does. Winchester, by the way, was named in 1809 for James Winchester, captain in the Revolutionary Army.

4. DOWNTOWN HUNTSVILLE STREETS

Huntsville of 1810 consisted of 20 square blocks. The streets were named for patriots of the day - the city hadn't existed long enough to name them for community leaders or favorite sons. Most of the original streets and their positions remain today.

ADAMS STREET. This street was added to the city in 1825. From 1821 to 1825, Henry Adams was editor of the local *Alabama Republican* newspaper and *Planters Magazine*. But there is no indication that the street was named for him. Instead it is more likely named for John Quincy Adams, who became U.S. President that same year.

John Quincy was son of Abigail and John Adams, the second U.S. President. He graduated from Harvard, got elected to the U.S. Congress. In 1817, President Monroe named him Secretary of State, and he negotiated cession of Florida from Spain. After his Presidency, he returned to the House of Representatives and served for 17 years, until he had a stroke and died in the Speaker's Room in 1848.

Adams Street might be best known among older Huntsvillians for the huge oak tree that once stood right in its middle. It was cut down in 1956, considered a hazard to automobile traffic. It had 201 rings, meaning it had started to grow in 1755, long before the city - even the country - was formed.

BANISTER ALLEY. It is one of three named alleys in the Twickenham Historic District, appears unpaved, and runs one block between Greene and Adams Streets. It is named for Dr. John Monro Banister, Episcopal minister of Church of the Nativity from 1850 to 1860, and then rector emeritus of that church from 1860 until his death in 1906.

CHURCH STREET. This is one of the city's earliest streets. It was apparently intended as a street for churches, hence its name, yet the city's biggest downtown churches were built elsewhere. Today on Church Street there are two churches: A stone in the wall of the Cumberland Presbyterian Church says the original was built in 1874, the church was reconstructed in 1909, and the last remodeling was in 1974. Across the street is St. John's African Methodist Episcopal Church. The stone on it tells that it was built in 1900, with its annex added in 1925.

CLINTON AVENUE. George Clinton was the first Governor of New York, a post he held for 21 years. He was the longest serving governor of a state until Iowa governor Terry Branstad surpassed him in 2015.

In 1804, Clinton became President Jefferson's running mate, replacing Aaron Burr. He became the fourth vice president of the United States. He again served as vice president under President Madison. He was the first of only two vice presidents to serve in the position under two different presidents - John C. Calhoun was the other.

Clinton was vice president when Madison County and Huntsville were formed.

CRUSE ALLEY. It is the longest and widest of the three alleys in the Twickenham Historic District. Sam Ridley Cruse was mayor of Huntsville in 1831 and 1832. He was also secretary and treasurer of the Memphis and Charleston Railroad. His 1825 home stands on Adams Street at Cruse Alley.

DAVIS CIRCLE. A traffic roundabout just north of the HMC Library, it's named for astronaut Dr. Nancy Jan Davis, Huntsville High graduate, who holds degrees from Auburn, Georgia Tech, and UAH. She was mission specialist on the 50th space shuttle mission in 1992, performed experiments in the spacehab (space habitation module) in 1994, and was payload commander on the 12-day Discovery mission in 1997. She totaled 673 hours in space. Davis retired from NASA in 2005.

ECHOLS AVENUE. Following the land sale of 1809 in which he bought much of the land that would later become downtown Huntsville, LeRoy Pope selected the highest hill overlooking the town as the site for his home. The home, one of the great antebellum mansions of Alabama (and still standing), was sold to Charles Hayes Patton and inherited by his daughter who married Major William Holding Echols. Echols had been born in Huntsville in 1834, graduated from West Point, and served with the Confederacy as a major of engineers at Charleston. After the war Echols farmed cotton, was connected with the Bell Factory, and was president of the First National Bank. He died in 1909.

Echols Avenue cuts across what was originally part of the Pope site. You would think that the hill would be named Pope Hill, but it is commonly known instead as Echols Hill.

EUSTIS AVENUE. The avenue is named for William Eustis. A surgeon from Massachusetts, Eustis served in the Revolutionary War, served in the U.S. House of Representatives, then became Secretary of War under President Madison. He attempted to prepare the Army before the War of 1812, but had to resign in the face of criticism following American reverses on the battlefield. He went on to become minister to Holland, regained his seat in the House, finally served as Governor of Massachusetts.

Part of what is now Eustis Avenue was once named Maiden Lane, which reportedly got its name because the street led to the nearby Huntsville Female Seminary, and its students regularly walked what was then indeed just a lane.

4. Downtown Huntsville Streets

FRANKLIN STREET. It is named for Benjamin Franklin - publisher, author, scientist, politician, and statesman.

Franklin was born in 1706. By 20 he owned his own press, publishing the *Pennsylvania Gazette* (later *The Saturday Evening Post*), and had begun writing *Poor Richard's Almanack*. He also served as clerk to the Pennsylvania Assembly, ran a book store, and undertook numerous scientific experiments - inventing the Franklin stove (more efficient than a fireplace) and proving (through his famous kite experiment) that lightning is electricity. Franklin was 46 when he began his political career. In 1757 he went to England as an agent, and by 1776 knew more about America than anyone in England, and more about England than anyone in America. He served in the Continental Congress and helped draft the Declaration of Independence. He became a minister to France, securing its aid, and by 1783, he, John Adams, and John Jay obtained the peace treaty that guaranteed national independence. In 1787 he attended the Constitutional Convention and urged ratification of the Constitution and inauguration of the new government under his friend George Washington. Franklin died in 1790.

GALLATIN STREET is named for Swiss immigrant Albert Gallatin. He was elected senator from Pennsylvania but couldn't serve because he hadn't been a citizen long enough. He went on to serve in the U.S. House of Representatives, and as Secretary of the Treasury from 1801 to 1812, minister to France from 1816 to 1823, then president of the National Bank of New York. Gallatin was also an expert on American Indian languages and president of the New York Historical Society.

Treasury Secretary Gallatin was a member of the commission Jefferson sent to purchase Georgia lands that created the Mississippi Territory of which Madison County would be a part.

GATES AVENUE. The avenue is named for General Horatio Gates. In 1772 this former Englishman settled in Virginia, and when the Revolutionary War began, he immediately volunteered in the Continental Army, serving as Adjutant General. In the field, he forced British surrender at Saratoga, but was later defeated at the battle of Camden, South Carolina. He ended the war working at Washington's headquarters, then freed his slaves and retired to New York.

GREENE STREET. Although it was originally spelled "Green" (and some maps and signs still read that way), the street was named for Revolutionary War hero Nathaniel Greene. During the Revolutionary War, Rhode Islander Greene was made a brigadier general and served with Washington from 1775 to 1778, acting informally as second in command. In 1781 Greene outmaneuvered Cornwallis to win the Southern campaign. After the war he was given land by the State of Georgia and lived the rest of his life in Savannah.

HOLMES AVENUE. The avenue is not named for Oliver Wendell Holmes, as many people guess (and not for Sherlock Holmes either). It is named for David Holmes.

David Holmes grew up in Virginia and in 1797 was elected to the U.S. Congress where he served six consecutive terms. In 1809, President Jefferson appointed Holmes Governor of the Mississippi Territory, of which Madison County was a part. He succeeded Robert Willliams and served as Territorial Governor from 1809 to 1817. When Mississippi became a state, Holmes became its first Governor.

JEFFERSON STREET. It is named for Thomas Jefferson, one of the most remarkable of the men of the Revolutionary era.

Jefferson was born in Virginia in 1743, attended William and Mary College, and embarked on a political career. In 1774 he wrote resolutions blaming England for its treatment of the colonies, and was asked to (and did) draft the Declaration of Independence. Jefferson succeeded Patrick Henry as Virginia Governor, then in 1789 was named Washington's Secretary of State. In 1796 he ran for President, but came in second to John Adams, thus becoming Vice President. In 1800 he ran again, beat Adams, but tied in the electoral college with Aaron Burr. When Congress broke the tie in his favor, he became the third President of the United States. In 1803 he took perhaps his most important action when he purchased the Louisiana Territory from Napoleon, doubling the country's size.

Jefferson was President from 1801 to 1809 during which the Mississippi Territory and Madison County were created.

After his Presidency, Jefferson retired to Monticello where there are many examples of his inventiveness: a weathervane that can be read inside, a clock with faces inside and out, dumbwaiters, and his bed that could be raised when not in use. He devised a copy machine, invented a revolving music stand, improved agriculture. He read classics in their original French, Spanish, Italian, or Greek. He conceived the University of Virginia, got it located in his own county, designed its buildings, hired the faculty, and served as its first regent.

In one of the great coincidences of history, Jefferson and John Adams both died on the same day - July 4, 1823 - exactly 50 years after the signing of the Declaration of Independence.

LINCOLN STREET. This street appears to have been named for Attorney General Levi Lincoln, a Harvard lawyer from Massachusetts. In 1800 he was elected to Congress and served until March 1801 when President Jefferson appointed him Attorney General. He held the office until 1805, after which he became lieutenant governor and later governor of Massachusetts. He died in 1820.

During his time as Attorney General he was part of the commission that Jefferson sent to purchase lands claimed by the state of Georgia. Purchase by the U.S. government created the northern portion of the Mississippi Territory of which Madison County became a part.

(In the 2003-5 editions of this book I attributed Lincoln Street to Benjamin Lincoln, major general in the Continental Army who was said to have led the army to Yorktown and the British surrender that ended the Revolutionary War. That appears to have been a good guess, but an incorrect one.)

LOWE AVENUE. Lowes have been active in the city from its earliest days. Bartlett M. Lowe was a merchant, the rector of the Huntsville Military Scientific and Classical School that opened in 1832, and president of the Huntsville branch of the Bank of the State of Alabama in 1835. William Manning Lowe was born in Huntsville in 1842, was a member of the Alabama Legislature in 1870, and served in the U.S. House of Representatives from 1879 until his death in 1882. Lawyer Robert Joseph Lowe was also born in Huntsville, in 1861, was a member of the Alabama Legislature from 1886 to 1889, and helped write the state constitution of 1901.

There are still more successful Lowes who could be included here. It must have been just a popular name, as I haven't found a record of Lowe Avenue being named to honor any specific one of the above.

MADISON STREET. Like the county, the street is named for James Madison, the fourth President of the United States, who served from 1809 to 1817. One of Madison's first actions in 1809 was to have a census of Madison County conducted, followed by the first government sale of land that became the city of Huntsville.

4. Downtown Huntsville Streets

Madison was born in Virginia in 1751, went to what is now Princeton University. He served on the Virginia council of state under Governors Patrick Henry and Thomas Jefferson, and in 1779 was elected to the Continental Congress. By the time he retired in 1783, he was thought of as its most effective legislator. He was an advocate of a strong central government, strong executive, independent court system, and bicameral legislature, with built-in checks and balances. He's known as the "Father of the Constitution" and is credited with wording much of it. In 1808 he succeeded Jefferson to the Presidency, and was re-elected in 1812, leading the country through its war with Britain. Madison died in 1836.

MCCLUNG AVENUE. The avenue was opened in 1825 and named for James White McClung. He was educated in Tennessee and North Carolina. As soon as he received his law degree, he settled in Huntsville. At various times from 1822 to 1844, he was a member of the Alabama Legislature, and from 1835 to 1838 he was Speaker of the House. Then from 1845 to his death in 1849, McClung served in the Alabama Senate. This was the first Huntsville street named for a local person.

MONROE STREET. Damill Castello Monroe came to Huntsville in 1886. He married Elizabeth Strove in 1892, and they had four sons. The family became well known in Huntsville for operating Monroe Printing Company, Monroe Office Supply, and subsequent endeavors. Although their businesses were nearby, according to historians, Monroe Street is not named for this local Monroe family.

The street, like others downtown, is named for a U.S. president, in this case, President James Monroe, who held that office from 1817 to 1825. Monroe fought in the Revolutionary War, studied law under Thomas Jefferson, and served as U.S. Senator from, and as Governor of, Virginia. President Jefferson sent Monroe to France to negotiate purchase of New Orleans only to have him find Napoleon ready to sell the entire Louisiana Territory; a quick negotiation was completed. President Madison named Monroe Secretary of State, later Secretary of War. As President, Monroe is best known for the Monroe Doctrine, supporting the independence of Spain's Latin American colonies. Monroe died in 1831.

Monroe was the last of the Revolutionary War heroes to serve high office.

NEAL ALLEY. One of three alleys in the Twickenham Historic District, it is named for Stephen Neal, appointed sheriff by Robert Williams in 1808, a position he held until Alabama became a state in 1819, at which time Neal was elected sheriff over 18 opponents.

RANDOLPH STREET/AVENUE is named for John Randolph of Virginia. Randolph was elected to the U.S. House of Representatives in 1799 where he served almost continuously for 30 years. He was a noted orator, advocate of states' rights, and a supporter of slavery.

SPRAGINS STREET. The street runs north from the Big Spring and is named for one of Huntsville's oldest and most recognized families. About 1820, Malchijah E. Spragins, with his brother Stith Bolling Spragins, moved with his mother Rebecca Bolling Spragins into Madison County, near Huntsville.

Perhaps most famous - maybe typical - of the Spragins family is Malchijah's grandson, Robert Elias Spragins, born in 1861. A lawyer, banker, businessman, and county attorney, he formed the Huntsville Ice and Coal Company, took over the Huntsville Electric Light and Power Company, bought the Huntsville Gas Company, was a major investor in the Lincoln Mill, and was director of the First National Bank - to name just some of his business affairs. In 1901 he was named to the state constitutional convention. In 1903 he was elected state senator and served four consecutive terms. In the 1920s, he was president of the State Highway Commission. He was repeatedly urged to run for Governor, but declined. Robert E. Spragins died in 1935.

WASHINGTON STREET. The street is named for George Washington (1732-1799).

Washington was a Virginia farmer, surveyor, colonel during the French and Indian War, commander of the Continental Army during the Revolutionary War, political leader afterwards, chairman of the Constitutional Convention, and first President of the United States. Washington served two terms before retiring to his home at Mount Vernon. His achievements as President include building the executive branch of the government, and selecting the site for the capital city that bears his name.

WILLIAMS STREET is named for Robert Williams, who was Governor of the Mississippi Territory from 1805 to 1809. It was Williams who made the proclamation on December 13, 1808, that created Madison County as part of the Territory.

5. STREETS IN HUNTSVILLE'S FIVE POINTS DISTRICT

In the 1880s, Huntsville was a small town of less than 5,000 people, still suffering from the Reconstruction that followed the Civil War. But it had a potential for growth, and local businessmen joined together to take that message to northern industrialists. Two in particular responded: the O'Shaughnessy brothers. In 1886 they, along with eighteen local business investors, organized the North Alabama Improvement Company. It was a pioneer organization similar to today's Chamber of Commerce in its promotion of the city and its businesses. It was also a corporation designed to make money through real estate ventures. One such venture was the acquisition of 2,000 acres for an East Huntsville Addition. The area was platted in 1888, and by 1889, lots were sold.

About that time, three businessmen from South Dakota came to Huntsville. They were Tracy W. Pratt, Willard I. Wellman, and William S. Wells. In South Dakota they, along with James A. Ward, had formed the Northwestern (sometimes written North West) Land Association. The Association bought almost the entire East Huntsville Addition from the North Alabama Improvement Company - almost all because it did not include a western portion that had been deeded to Dallas Mill.

The Addition was re-platted in 1892. The avenues that ran east and west were named for Company directors and prominent local citizens; streets that ran north and south were numbered. The avenues retain most of their original 1892 names today. The streets, on the other hand, got their names in the Ordinance of 1958 that renamed roads throughout the city. Many of the people whose names are on the streets have nothing to do with Five Points history but still provide brief stories of interest.

The three "Yankee businessmen" were joined in their endeavors by three local men, Milton Humes, J.R. Stevens, and Charles H. Halsey. Elizabeth Chapman in her book writes about the group: "They were a city-building and manufacturing group. ... The history of the next eight years is permeated with their ideas. There is hardly an important transaction that they do not direct, not all of them at once, but some of them all the time. Their names appear as agents to secure mills for the Chamber of Commerce, as realtors, developing waste lands or destroying old property for new business. They appear as chairmen of town meetings, and finally, as the directors and presidents of the Chamber of Commerce."

The East Huntsville Five Points area of today gets its name from the intersection of Andrew Jackson Way, Pratt Avenue, and Holmes Avenue and the five points of land they create.

ANDREW JACKSON WAY. (Originally 5th Street) This major street through Five Points is named for Andrew Jackson, seventh President of the United States, who served from 1829 to 1837. Long before that, General Jackson acquired a lot of land in Madison County, and frequently visited the area. He particularly liked the Old Green Bottom Inn where he "raced his horses and fought his cocks." Site of that inn is now part of Alabama A&M University.

BEIRNE AVENUE. The 1892 plat map of the East Huntsville Addition, developed by the Northwestern Land Association, shows Bierne Avenue. An old postcard shows the Bierne home. Both are apparently misspellings. The correct name is Beirne.

In 1793, Andrew O'Beirne came to Virginia from Ireland, and dropped the O. He married Elener Kenan, and they had seven children, one of whom was George. I'm told the street is probably named for George.

41

5. Streets in Huntsville's Five Points District

In 1842, by then in Huntsville, George Plunket Beirne was elected alderman, then the next year elected mayor. For 1849 and 1850, he was re-elected mayor. He was a director of the Northern Bank of Alabama, later the First National Bank of Huntsville. He was also on the board of the Memphis and Charleston Railroad. He owned a fine home on Williams Street and land south of the city. George died in 1881 at age 72.

According to the family history, he married Eliza G. Carter (Fred Simpson in *The Sins of Madison County* lists her as Eliza Carter Gray), and they had a daughter, Jane. She inherited George's home and land. But she never married. She lived until 1918.

One Beirne family write-up (by Martha Patton Darwin) says George had nine children, but provides no details or dates. Another (by William Echols Spragins) says that since George had no son, the Beirne family in Alabama ended with spinster daughter Jane. She died in 1918.

COLEMAN STREET. (Originally 7th Street) Daniel Coleman was born in Athens in 1838. He served in the Confederate Army, was a state senator, then resigned to practice law in Huntsville. He was elected for six years as solicitor of the Eighth Judicial Circuit by the general assembly. In 1884 he was president of the Alabama Bar Association.

DALLAS STREET. Dallas Street and the Dallas Mill from which it took its name are not directly connected with Dallas, Texas - although the name is from the same Dallas family. Dallas Mill in Huntsville was named after its principal stockholder, Trevanion B. Dallas of Nashville. The mill began operation in 1892 and was Alabama's largest cotton mill, manufacturing sheeting. Dallas was treasurer and general manager of the facility until 1902. The mill operated until 1949. Nothing of it remains today but for a water tower with Dallas Mill printed on it, at the north end of Dallas Street.

George Dallas, for whom the Texas city is named, was Trevanion's uncle.

ENGLAND STREET. (Originally 8th Street) Dr. Walter Booker England was from Tennessee. After obtaining his Doctor of Medicine degree, he set up practice in Huntsville. His office was at the corner of Randolph Avenue and East Side Square. His home was on East Holmes. He is credited with diagnosing the first case of Spanish Flu in Alabama. Unfortunately he was caught in the 1918 epidemic himself and died at age 36.

A Gilbert H. England (a descendent?) was assistant postmaster in the 1950s and it could be that England Street was named for him rather than the original Dr. England.

GRAYSON STREET. (Originally 11th Street) John Grayson arrived in Huntsville in 1807. He had been appointed by President Jefferson to aid Thomas Freeman in the original survey of Madison County. He was a trustee of the Green Academy and owned the Flint River Navigation Company. He and his family lived in the Big Cove area.

Grayson Street is known as "where the sidewalks end" from the fact that in 1925 when the East Huntsville area was finally annexed into the city, Grayson Street was its Eastern boundary.

HALSEY AVENUE. Charles H. Halsey and his brother William Leroy opened their grocery business in 1879. It continues in business today under the name Halsey Foodservice. (See 8. Halsey Grocery.)

Charles Halsey was general manager of the North Alabama Improvement Company. Later he was one of the three local businessmen who joined in the Northwestern Land Association partnership.

5. Streets in Huntsville's Five Points District

HUMES AVENUE. Three local businessmen joined in the Northwestern Land Association partnership. Lawyer Milton Humes was one. He served as the group's only attorney.

Humes was originally from Virginia and had come to Huntsville after the Civil War. He had been a Confederate captain and had lost both of his legs fighting General Sherman. He was admitted to the bar in 1866, practiced law in Huntsville all his life, and was twice president of the state bar association. He died in 1908.

LACY STREET. (Originally 9th Street) Theophilus Lacy was cashier of the Northern Bank of Alabama in 1859. The bank closed during the Civil War and re-opened in 1865 as the National Bank of Huntsville. Lacy was its cashier until 1874.

MCCULLOUGH AVENUE. Augustus W. McCullough was an investor and participant in the North Alabama Improvement Company. Patricia Ryan wrote (in her 1983 Planning Department Report, *Northern Dollars for Huntsville Spindles*) that McCullough was a Huntsville court clerk. Elise Stephens (in *Historic Huntsville – A City of New Beginnings*) wrote about him as a member of the executive committee of the local labor union and as "a school teaching carpetbagger with staying power who made the transition from bagger to community builder." For 1870-1871, he was a trustee for Alabama A&M. The 1896-1897 city directory lists him as U.S. Commissioner and special master, Memphis and Charleston Railroad, with home on Meridian Pike.

MCKINLEY AVENUE. This is the northern most street in the Five Points area before Oakwood Avenue. The avenue was originally platted as Melette Avenue, named after the governor of South Dakota, but the name was changed to honor President William McKinley (1843-1901), 25th President of the United States. McKinley had won re-election in the election of 1900 and was inaugurated again in March 1901. That same year, in April, McKinley's train stopped in Huntsville, and a large crowd

44

greeted the President. Then in September, McKinley went to Buffalo, New York, to attend the Pan American Exhibition. He was shot there by an anarchist and died eight days later.

MINOR STREET. (Originally 10th Street) When delegates met to write the Alabama constitution in 1819, Madison County had eight delegates, one of which was Henry Minor. In 1817 Minor had been attorney general of the Mississippi Territory, and during 1818-1819 he served as clerk of the Madison County Court. He later served as clerk of the Alabama Supreme Court from 1825 until his death in 1838.

O'SHAUGHNESSY AVENUE. It wasn't until the 1870s that industrialized textile manufacturing, i.e., the big cotton mills, came to Huntsville. Michael and James F. O'Shaughnessy's father had made a fortune in Cincinnati, and his two sons came to Nashville where they built one of the South's first cottonseed oil factories. In 1881, they opened the Huntsville Cotton Oil Mill and eventually controlled oil mills throughout Alabama, had a refinery in Brooklyn, and shipped oil as far away as Europe.

It was Michael who moved to Huntsville and built the home known as Kildare where he had foxhounds and horses. (Kildare was later sold to the Cyrus McCormick family and known for some time as the McCormick House. It still stands, a block from Oakwood Avenue and Meridian Pike.)

In 1886 the brothers along with local businessmen formed the North Alabama Improvement Company. In 1890, with "outside" financing, the group brought Dallas Mill to the city. But also by 1890, O'Shaughnessy expenses were overrunning income. James had, for example, invested heavily in building a failing canal across Nicaragua. In 1892 the brothers had to sell out, in a six million dollar deal, to the Northwestern Land Association run by South Dakota businessmen Pratt, Ward, Wellman, and Wells. At this point Michael and his family left the city.

5. Streets in Huntsville's Five Points District

PRATT AVENUE. Tracy Wilder Pratt was born in 1861, grew up in Minnesota, and later moved to Pierre, South Dakota, where he became a newspaper editor, successful real estate and insurance man, even state representative. He moved to Huntsville in the 1890s and lived here until his death in 1928. He was vice president of the Northwestern Land Association.

Typical of Pratt was his forming a company to create the city's first rail (street car) line from west side to Dallas Mill. Its stock was valued at $100,000. Pratt invested $99,700.

Pratt's obituary stated "he was responsible for more major industries locating in Huntsville than any other man who ever resided here, and he was often called 'Huntsville's First Citizen.' He was a member of and identified with practically every civic, social, fraternal, patriotic, and business organization in Huntsville." Lane Lambert summed him up as "the founder of one cotton mill, a force behind two others, the principal investor in the city's first public transportation [street car] service, and a sort of one-man Chamber of Commerce for the town."

RISON AVENUE. The W.R. Rison Banking Company went into business in 1866, weathered the bank panic of 1873, and grew to be the largest bank in the city. Rison was serving as its president in 1900. When Trevanion Dallas died in 1902, Rison became manager of the Dallas Mill. In 1904, he was succeeded by his son, Archie L. Rison, who held the post until 1925.

William R. Rison was also vice-president of the Huntsville Land Company, which developed the land near Dallas Mill for residential use. Oscar Goldsmith was that company's president, and the development was originally named Lawrence Village for Goldsmith's young son. (See Goldsmith-Schiffman Field.)

RUSSELL STREET. (Originally 6th Street) The street was re-named in 1958 as Russel Street, apparently for Albert Russel (see 12. Russel Hill). The city has misspelled it (2 Ls) ever since.

STEVENS AVENUE. Three local businessmen joined in the Northwestern Land Association partnership. J. R. Stevens, ex-Confederate major, was one. He had become president of the National Bank of Huntsville in 1882, and had been treasurer of the North Alabama Improvement Company.

WARD AVENUE. James A. Ward was one of the group of South Dakotans who formed the Northwestern Land Association. Ward was a lawyer and railroad speculator. He served as the group's treasurer. Of the four South Dakotans, he is the one who never moved to Huntsville.

WELLMAN AVENUE. Willard I. Wellman, like Tracy Pratt, was from Minnesota but moved to South Dakota where he allied himself with Pratt and became a successful real estate and insurance man. He moved to Huntsville with Pratt and Wells. He served as secretary of the Northwestern Land Association.

Wellman was also the first president of the Farmers and Merchants Bank, owned a furniture company, bought and sold real estate throughout the county, and formed the Boyd & Wellman real estate firm that subdivided lots and constructed housing. In the early twentieth century, Wellman also served as chairman of the state Republican Party.

WELLS AVENUE runs along the north side of Maple Hill Cemetery. William S. Wells hailed from Elmira, New York, but moved to Pierre, South Dakota. He owned the Wells House there, and was president of the Pierre, Duluth, and Black Hills Railway. He moved to Huntsville with Pratt and Wellman, and was president of the Northwestern Land Association. Wells' impact on Huntsville was limited, as he died in 1900. His obituary stated that "he was a banker, contractor, builder, stock raiser, and livery man."

6. MORE HUNTSVILLE STREETS

AIRPORT ROAD. Airport Road leads to John Hunt Park and several city buildings, all of which occupy the area of the old Huntsville airport. The old airport served the area until the 1970s - with long-gone carriers like Capitol Airlines, Southern Airways, and Eastern Airlines.

ALAN B. SHEPARD HIGHWAY. Interstate 565 in Huntsville has been named the Admiral Alan B. Shepard Highway.

Alan Bartlett Shepard, Jr., was born in New Hampshire in 1923 and graduated from the U.S. Naval Academy in 1944. He served on a destroyer in World War II, and afterwards took flight training and became a test pilot. In 1959, he was chosen as one of the first group of astronauts. On May 17, 1961, Shepard became the first American in space by traveling up 117 miles atop a Redstone rocket in the Freedom 7 capsule. In 1971 he went on to captain Apollo 14 and conduct geological experiments on the surface of the moon. That same year he was made a rear admiral, first astronaut to be awarded that high a rank. Shepard died in 1998.

BAILEY COVE ROAD. Joseph Franklin Bailey was born in 1816 in the Mississippi Territory. He married Frances Maria Flippo in 1841. By 1850 they were listed as living in Madison County. They had eight sons, of which Lewis Winston Bailey, born in 1845, was one. He married Georgian Mary M. McCay in 1868. In 1879 the couple purchased 287 acres due east of the original Four Mile Post Road, and it is for this couple and that place that Bailey Cove is named. Lewis Bailey died in 1924.

BANKHEAD PARKWAY. This road on the north side of Monte Sano Mountain is named for William Bankhead.

John Hollis Bankhead (1842-1920), from Lamar County, Alabama, served as a Confederate captain, later became U.S. Representative from 1887 to 1907, then U.S. Senator from Alabama from 1907 to his death in 1920. Among his achievements, he helped develop the U.S. highway system and as a result had his name given to the first transcontinental road across the country from Washington, D.C., to San Diego, California: the Bankhead Highway. One son, John Hollis, Jr. (1872-1946), also from Lamar County and a lawyer, was elected to the U.S. Senate in 1930 and served there the rest of his life.

But it was the first son, William Brockman Bankhead, who in 1895 came to Huntsville to practice law. He was elected to the U.S. House of Representatives in 1916 while his father was Senator - an unprecedented event. In 1933 he chaired the House Rules Committee, by 1934 he was Majority Leader, and in 1936 he became Speaker of the House. In 1940, just before his death, he was keynote speaker at the Democratic National Convention.

William had two daughters, one of whom was actress Tallulah Brockman Bankhead, born in Huntsville in 1903.

BIDE-A-WEE DRIVE. When I mentioned I was working on this book, someone said he sure wished I'd include and explain northeast Huntsville's Bide-A-Wee Drive. So here it is. It's Scottish, and to a Scot, the name means "stay a little longer" or "linger awhile." A literal translation might be "stay a while."

BLEVINS GAP ROAD. Dillon Blevins and sons John and William arrived in the area in the early 1800s, and in 1809 the sons bought land along what is now Whitesburg Drive. They bought more land in 1810 and 1811, including some east of Green Mountain in Little Cove. Then the family bought the gap for easy access across the mountains between their lands. There are references to people crossing at the gap as early as the 1820s, and the road is clearly shown on the Madison County map of

1850. For many years it continued as the main road east over the mountains. Almost 200 years later, Huntsville's latest road in that area, Cecil Ashburn Drive, uses the same mountain gap.

BLUE SPRINGS ROAD. An 1861 Hartley-Drayton map shows a branch, labeled Blue Spring Branch, of the creek that flowed just west of downtown - what is today called Pinhook Creek. An 1865 military map shows what appears to be a pond labeled Blue Spring in the same location - west of the city between Holmes and Clinton Streets. Since no Blue family appears in the census records around that time, the spring must have been named for its color. Blue Springs Road has its southern terminus at Oakwood Avenue, far north of today's Holmes Avenue, but still likely takes its name from the spring or springs that once existed.

BOB WALLACE AVENUE. Local lore has long said that Bob Wallace was a nephew of developer's sister, but nothing more was known. In 2014 author Linda Allen figured it out:

Edward L. Pulley was a Huntsville lawyer turned entrepreneur. In 1908 he, his sister Jimmie, and his brother-in-law Nathaniel Wallace incorporated as the South Huntsville Development Company. Within a year they had laid out land west of Whitesburg Drive from Marshuetz Avenue on the north to what was already called Bob Wallace Avenue on the south. Nathaniel had married another of Pulley's sisters, Mary, in 1893, and they had had a son, Robert Pulley Wallace born in 1898 in Tennessee. That's the Bob for whom the street was named. Bob attended Vanderbilt University and became a successful doctor, practicing in Manhattan with an office on Park Avenue. He died in 1957. He never lived in Huntsville.

Allen concludes the local lore was correct. Bob Wallace was indeed a nephew of two developers, Edward L. Pulley and his sister Jimmie.

BRAC CIRCLE. West of Zierdt Road on the west side of Redstone Arsenal is this reminder of Base Realignment and Closure. BRAC was a Department of Defense process that closed 350 military installations from 1988 through 2005. Redstone was one of the beneficiaries. This street named circle - actually a cul-de-sac - stands amidst new home developments created for families many of whom relocated here as a result of BRAC.

BYRD SPRING ROAD. Byrd Spring is part of the Indian Creek waterway that runs from Big Spring to the Tennessee River, and this South Huntsville road runs west from Whitesburg Drive to the woods that surround the spring.

The Strobridge & Co. map of 1875 clearly has the area marked "Bird's Spring." An article in *Old Huntsville* magazine (No. 95) tells of a body being found at "Bird's Spring" on land owned by S.W. Harris in 1888. The *Weekly Community Newspaper* of March 2, 1922, tells when a group of 25 businessmen, with Jeff Terry, treasurer, organized the "Bird Spring Gun and Rodd Club" by buying over 400 acres at the site (but not the spring itself), owned by Robert Crawford of Fayetteville. When or why the "i" got changed to a "y" is unclear.

John Hays told me the story of the road itself: Between 1910 and 1920, land south of the spring was owned by Elgie Hays. It was rented to a logger who set up a saw mill and used oxen to access the marsh and its stand of tupelo trees. To make a road in and out, he felled trees on one side of the would-be road to fall onto the road site, and cut trees on the other side that way too, so that the fallen trees criss-crossed. Dirt was packed down on top, thus forming a log causeway into the marsh - and the start of today's Byrd Spring Road.

From what I could find, no one named Bird or Byrd ever owned the land at or around the spring. Indeed, courthouse records show that lands in the area were originally purchased in 1809 and 1812 by someone named Peregrin Falconer, certainly a bird-like name. Yet Falconer was not as strange a name as it might sound. In 1820 Joshua Falconer was one of the original businessmen on the courthouse square, with a business at the corner of South Side Square and Madison Street.

CALIFORNIA STREET. In the introduction to *Maple Hill Cemetery, Phase One*, Frances Roberts wrote "Forced to sell land by pressing creditors, ... LeRoy Pope Walker was directed by the court to divide much of his Uncle's [sic] property adjacent to the City into lots and streets. This appears to be the origins of White and California Streets."

Dr. Roberts was addressing the cemetery layout, not the specific street names. Still, the year was 1849, year of the California gold rush. Unlike White Street, on which Thomas W. White resided, there was no one by the name of California. It's a guess that gold rush fever and perhaps wishful thinking hit someone in Huntsville at that time to produce this street name.

CARL T. JONES DRIVE. George Washington Jones served as a major in the Confederate army. A year after the war ended, a son, George Walter Jones, known as G.W., was born. In 1886, G.W. founded the civil engineering firm that bears his name. In 1890 G.W. married Elvalena Moore, and they had five sons and a daughter.

About 1939, sons Edwin and Carl purchased the 2500-acre Garth farm and its 1823 house south of Huntsville, an area now known as Jones Valley. After World War II they made the farm a success, raising cattle (originally brought in from Texas) and producing seed (Certified Ky-31 Fescue). In the 1950s and 1960s Carl also served as one of the partners of G.W. Jones & Sons, did engineering projects, and became a dynamic community leader especially recognized for bringing industries to

Huntsville. One of the engineering efforts for which Carl was particularly recognized is design of the Huntsville International Airport field, which is named for him.

Carl T. Jones Drive crosses Jones Valley, connecting Airport Road with Bailey Cove Road.

CECIL ASHBURN DRIVE. Cecil Ashburn grew up learning about roads - his grandfather was one of Madison County's early road commissioners. Then during World War II, Ashburn served with the Army Corps of Engineers and Seabees. When the war was over, it was no surprise when he got into the road construction business. In 1946, he and his uncle, Pat Gray, formed Ashburn & Gray. From the 1950s to 1970s, the firm built many of the area streets and roads traveled today - Memorial Parkway, most of University Drive, some of I-565, the roads at Huntsville International Airport and even its runways - to name a few. Perhaps the toughest was Governors Drive, over rocky Monte Sano, to where Hampton Cove is now. When the latest road in that direction, Four Mile Post Road Extended, was completed, the city named it in honor of Cecil Ashburn. Gray died in 1970, Ashburn in 2012.

CECIL FAIN DRIVE. The road crosses Winchester Road just west of Blue Springs Road. It is named for Cecil Vincent Fain, Huntsville teacher, coach, and principal for over 50 years. Fain served as principal at eight schools, including Lee High School, but is best remembered as principal of Rison High School, where he served for 32 years. Several area firsts are attributed to him: first student safety patrol, state spelling bee, PTA, Boy Scout troop - even the county's first American Legion Post. Fain also coached - baseball, football, basketball, track, and tennis. Indeed, for 40 years, he was known locally as "Mr. Tennis." Cecil Fain died in 1992 at age 96.

CLOPTON STREET. It's two blocks west of, and parallel to

Triana Road. It's not a major thoroughfare, but it's worth noting because its name honors Anne Bradshaw Clopton, one of the city's most famous artists. Starting as a teenager in the 1890s, Anne successfully captured spider webs and developed a dot-by-dot technique of painting on them. She exhibited at the 1896 St. Louis World's Fair, in the 1930s and 1940s was featured on CBS radio, and demonstrated her paintings at the 1939 New York World's Fair. By the time of her death in 1956, Anne had painted over 600 cobweb pictures. Some remain in private collections. The Burritt Museum has several, but they are so fragile they are no longer on regular public display.

COOK AVENUE. Cook has been a common name in both Huntsville and Madison County. Perhaps the first Cook here was John Cook, who came to the County from South Carolina with his wife Margaret Shackleford in 1808.

The present three-block-long street is home to the Madison County Farmers Market. It would make a good story if the avenue was named for the cooks who came to the Farmers Market but it doesn't seem to be the case. The avenue got its name when the ordnance of 1958 renamed streets throughout Huntsville, and the Farmers Market didn't move to Cook Avenue from the Big Spring area until 1960. The name was apparently arbitrarily selected.

CRINER ROAD. Isaac and his uncle Joseph Criner are credited with being the first permanent settlers in Madison County. In 1805 they built cabins for their families in what is now New Market. But they never got anything special named for them until the 1960s when a residential street was named Criner Road. It is only a couple blocks long, and runs a block west of Garth Road, between Carl T. Jones Drive and Four Mile Post Road.

DRAKE AVENUE. Revolutionary War soldier John Drake (of New Jersey) and his wife Jane Neely (from Virginia) had ten children, who gave them 68 grandchildren. John and family members moved to Madison County between 1807 and 1811, and by 1815 had purchased land in Drake's Cove, now known as Jones Valley.

Other members of the family settled east of Monte Sano, near what is now Big Cove - hence King Drake Road and Drake Mountain in that area. Some must have also owned land north of the city, as the mountain there that is being destroyed for gravel is another Drake Mountain.

Drakes owned land along the road in Huntsville that bears their name, as well as in the valley and further south along Whitesburg Drive. In 1881 the Drakes sold the valley farm to Winston W. Garth, and in 1940, Edwin and Carl Jones purchased it from the Garth estate. The original home on Garth Road, now owned by Jones descendants, was built by James Drake in the 1820s.

FEARN STREET. Going up Bankhead Parkway onto the north side of Monte Sano Mountain you will find it ends abruptly and becomes Fearn Street, named for the doctor who named the mountain.

FIGURES ALLEY. An alley in the Old Town Historic District running a block between Randolph and Clinton Avenues. William Bibb Figures was mayor of Huntsville 1854-55 and 1868-1870. He was also editor of the *Huntsville Advocate* newspaper from before the Civil War until his death in 1872.

FOUR MILE POST ROAD. The term "post road" can refer to a road used for the delivery of mail. The first such road in the country ran from Boston to New York in 1673. By the late 1700s, when Benjamin Franklin was Postmaster General, milestones were set out on routes run by post riders, as they were paid by the mile. But Four Mile Post Road is not a postal road.

The term can also refer to a road marked by a post or posts. Roads, with posts in place at regular intervals, were used by pioneers, especially in the north, where deep snow could obliterate trails without such manmade landmarks. Sans snow, there was such a post, on the northeast corner of the intersection of Four Mile Post Road and Whitesburg Drive, marking four miles from the courthouse in downtown Huntsville.

GARTH ROAD. Winston Fearn Garth was born in the Fearn-Garth home on Franklin Street in 1856, son of William Willis and Maria Fearn Garth. Winston graduated from University of the South at Sewanee and studied law at the University of Virginia, but because of his health, he had to retire.

In 1881 his father bought the Drake farm. In 1883 Winston married Lena Garth, daughter of Horace E. Garth, president of the Mechanics Bank of New York City. They lived in a new home that they called Piedmont on Whitesburg Drive, which was just over the hill from the farm. Winston became prominent as a breeder of harness horses. He also was active in politics, as chairman of the Madison County Democratic Committee, on the Governor's staff, and from 1922 to 1926, as state senator. He died in 1933.

In 1939 the farm was sold to the Jones family. Piedmont no longer exists - it burned down in the 1930s. Garth Road runs along the west side of what once was Garth farm, now known as Jones Valley.

GOVERNORS DRIVE. Some politicians wanted to name this avenue to honor Governor James E. "Big Jim" Folsom, but he declined and recommended it honor all Alabama governors. One newspaper write-up says it honors those governors who contributed to the building of roads in Madison County, another says it honors the nine Alabama governors who came from Madison County. For whatever purpose, Fifth Avenue was changed to Governors Drive in 1958.

HOBBS ROAD AND HOBBS ISLAND ROAD. These are named for early settler John Hobbs and the Hobbs family. (See 2. Hobbs Island.)

JAMES RECORD ROAD. This road runs across the north part of Huntsville International Airport.

In 1948 James Record was named county clerk auditor, the county's highest position at the time. From 1962 to 1981, he served four terms and 19 years as chairman of the Madison County Commission, at one time receiving the largest number of votes of anyone in county history. It was a time when thousands of new residents arrived to work at Redstone Arsenal and NASA, and the city and county successfully expanded services accordingly, including the opening of the airport, which was dedicated in 1968.

Upon retirement Record continued involvement on the boards of numerous charitable and state organizations, including the Alabama Historical Commission. One of his most lasting achievements was the writing of a history of Madison County. Record died in 1996 at age 79.

There are two other named roads at the airport. The roads in and out form the **Glenn Hearn Parkway**. A parallel road is **Houston Goodson Way**. Hearn was mayor of Huntsville and Goodson was president of the city council at the time the airport was built.

And at G.W. Jones & Sons, one of Carl T. Jones' most complicated engineering projects was that of designing the airport field, and for his success, the air field itself is named Carl T. Jones Field.

JORDAN LANE. According to a DAR paper in the Heritage

Room, this street was named for Bartholomew (Batt) Jordan, a Revolutionary War soldier and early settler. The paper goes on to say that Jordan died in 1842 and is buried in Jordan Cemetery on Redstone Arsenal, one of many small family cemeteries on the Arsenal.

DR. JOSEPH L. LOWERY BOULEVARD. A few blocks west of Huntsville Hospital, this north-south road between Governor's Drive and Williams Avenue has been called the gateway to downtown. It was opened in 2016 to honor Dr. Lowery, who was 94 at the time – and attended its dedication.

Lowery grew up in Huntsville. He co-founded the Southern Christian Leadership Conference with Dr. Martin Luther King, and later played a key role in the Montgomery bus boycott and in the Selma-to-Montgomery marches. He has since created the Joseph and Evelyn Lowery Institute for Justice and Human Rights in Atlanta.

L&N DRIVE. This road, a block east of Memorial Parkway, is a popular shortcut for drivers who want to travel from Bob Wallace Avenue, behind Parkway City Mall, to a point a mile south without getting on the parkway. It gets its name from the Louisville & Nashville Railroad, which once owned and ran on the adjacent track. In 1959 the railroad sold part of its right-of-way to the city so the road could be built.

By 1982, the L&N had become part of the Seaboard Coast Line, which then announced it was going to discontinue service through Huntsville. To keep service for industries in the Hobbs Island Road area, the Huntsville Madison County (HMC) Railroad Authority was created. In 1984, two weeks after abandonment by the Seaboard, the Railroad Authority purchased the property and assets of the line from Holmes Avenue to Hobbs Island Road. The 13.2-mile-long HMC rail line still operates today.

LEEMAN FERRY ROAD. The road is named for early settler William Lehman, who had stock pens, a ferry, and cabins on both sides of the Tennessee River a few miles below Ditto's Landing. An 1875 Madison County map (by Strobridge & Co., Cincinnati) shows a Leeman Ferry Road leading from Huntsville all the way to the Tennessee River, between Hobbs Island and Triana.

Usually spelled Leeman, his real name was Lehman, according to a *Huntsville Times* article by Lee Green. Also, TVA maps of the Tennessee River available via the Internet label an area nearby as Lehman's Bluff.

LILY FLAGG ROAD. One of Huntsville's legends is that, in 1892 Gen. Samuel H. Moore took his prize Jersey cow, Lily Flagg, to the Chicago World's Fair where it was pronounced the world's greatest butter producer, then returned home to hold a big celebration. But that version just isn't true.

Here's the real story: The cow was part of a dairy on Maysville Road in northeast Huntsville. To promote its breed, the American Jersey Cattle Club gave awards to its best producers. In 1892, club officials came to Huntsville and measured Lily Flagg's butter output (1,047 pounds that year) and named her champion butter producer. To celebrate her success, Moore, who owned the cow, really did hold a party in her honor. It was at his home on Adams Street. Formal invitations were sent, a greeting line extended past the cow that was on display, an orchestra played, and the party lasted until dawn. The following year, Moore took her to the Chicago World's Fair, but she was mishandled and didn't produce enough milk to enter competition. He sold her to a Massachusetts dairy, and she never returned to Huntsville.

The book of the fair, the Colombian Exposition of 1893, pictures "Lilly (Signal) Flag." But according to Doris Gilbreath's book

Lily Flagg, the cow's official name was "Signal's Lily Flagg."

Dr. David Moore had bought considerable land at the first land sales in the county in 1809. His son, Gen. Samuel H. Moore, eventually owned several plantations in the area. The son was also director of the Memphis-Chattanooga & St. Louis Railroad. When the railroad put a stop south of Huntsville, Moore named it after his cow, thus the area and road now known as Lily Flagg.

MARSHEUTZ AVENUE runs west from California Street to Huntsville High School, and between Governors Drive and Bob Wallace Avenue. Leo J. Marshuetz (sic) lived on Lincoln Street in the 1890s. He paid $100 for the first lot sold on the street that would ultimately bear his name. A few years later, he moved to Montgomery. Note that the city has misspelled his name.

MASTIN LAKE ROAD. Captain Francis T. Mastin was a planter who came to Alabama from Maryland as an aide to General Andrew Jackson during the Indian wars that followed the War of 1812. In 1823 Mastin bought a lot on Williams Street from Clement C. Clay for his home. He and his wife, Ann LeVert Mastin, had two sons, William and Ed, and by the mid-1800s, Mastins owned much land in both the city and county. Some of that land was north of Huntsville around the street that today bears their name.

And, yes, there had also been a lake there. It is no more - there's only a drainage ditch - but nearby names of Lakewood Park and Lakeview Drive attest to its one-time existence.

MAX LUTHER DRIVE. Max Agrippa Luther was born in Albertville in 1908. He moved to Huntsville in the mid-1930s. His home, on a couple hundred acres, was on Meridian Street next to the road that today bears his name.

Luther became one of the city's most successful cotton brokers.

6. More Huntsville Streets

The Max Luther Cotton Company was part of the old Cotton Row buildings on West Side Square. Luther did business with the New Orleans and Memphis Cotton Exchanges - so much so that when he died in 1955, the New Orleans Exchange closed for the day in his honor. Luther is buried in Maple Hill Cemetery.

Luther was an avid horseman. In the late 1940s he had a little mare called Sally Co-Ed that could do three gaits. He took her to shows in the Kentucky horse country where she won many times. He finally took her to Madison Square Garden in New York City. I'm told there's a photo of Luther and the mare at that show, Luther in tuxedo and the required derby, and all the attendees in formal dress. And that the trip with his little prize-winning mare made for one of his proudest moments.

MEDARIS DRIVE. Ohioan John Bruce Medaris served in the Marine Corps during World War I and in the Army Ordnance Corps during World War II. In 1955 he was promoted to major general and assigned as the first commanding general of the Army Ballistic Missile Agency at Redstone Arsenal. As such he led the team of German and American rocket engineers as the U.S. entered space in 1957 with the launch of the Explorer I satellite atop an Army Jupiter C missile.

In 1958 Medaris was made commanding general of the Ordnance Missile Command, which included not only all of Redstone Arsenal, but the White Sands Missile Range, Jet Propulsion Laboratory, and responsibility for all Army Ordnance rockets, guided and ballistic missiles, and space activities. That last resulted in Commander Alan B. Shepard being carried by a Mercury-Redstone on the first suborbital flight around the Earth.

Medaris retired from the military in 1960. In 1970, he became an Anglican priest, serving in North Carolina. He died in 1990 at age 88. He is buried in Arlington National Cemetery.

MEMORIAL PARKWAY. When it was first built in the 1950s and 1960s, the parkway honored soldiers killed during World War II. It now commemorates soldiers from all U.S. wars.

MERIDIAN STREET. Lands of Georgia originally extended all the way to the Mississippi River. In 1802, Georgia sold Mississippi Territory lands to the federal government. The territory had to be surveyed and platted before the lands could be opened for purchase under the administration of the federal government. Sometime between 1807 and 1809 the part of the territory that was to become Alabama was surveyed. Surveyor was Major Thomas Freeman, deputy U.S. surveyor. A base line or meridian had to be established for the state. It was known as the Huntsville Meridian, and part of it ran from the Tennessee border south to Huntsville along what is now U.S. 231 and the street that bears its name.

PATTON ROAD. Patton Road extends through Redstone Arsenal, north until it becomes Jordan Lane. It is named for the Patton family, which started here when William came from Virginia to start a merchandising business in 1812. He was a member of the firm Beirne & Patton, founded the Bell Factory, and operated his business as well as two plantations in Alabama and another in Mississippi. He and his wife, Martha Lee Hayes, had nine children.

Most of the Patton children became successful as planters and merchants. Charles Patton (1806-1866) became a Huntsville doctor. Most famous was Robert Miller Patton, educated at Green Academy, elected to the Alabama legislature, president of the Alabama Senate, and in 1865, elected Governor. Robert died in 1885.

Historians at Redstone Arsenal have a different source for the Patton Road name. See 14. Redstone Arsenal - CWS Roads.

6. More Huntsville Streets

PULASKI PIKE. This was one of the first roads in the county, and the only road between Huntsville and Pulaski, Tennessee, from which it takes its name.

Casimir Pulaski was a Lithuanian who had served in the Polish army, met Benjamin Franklin, and volunteered his services to the American cause in the Revolutionary War. He was made a brigadier general and commanded what became known as Pulaski's Legion. Pulaski was wounded and died at Savannah, Georgia.

SPARKMAN DRIVE. This major drive is named for Senator John J. Sparkman. (See 10. Sparkman High School for his story.)

ST. CLAIR AVENUE. St. Clair Lane, Place, Cemetery, and Drive, all off of Maysville Road in the eastern part of the county, are named for St. Clairs that settled in the Hurricane Creek valley area. George St. Clair was first to arrive, in the early 1800s. He and his wife had six sons and a daughter, and one of the sons, John Henry, got a wagon and mule and provided the area with its first rolling store. Later he built a store at what is now the intersection of County Lake and Hurricane Creek Roads. He eventually expanded further, owning thousands of acres of mountain land, running sawmill and coal businesses, then a gin that served the valley, finally a third store. John St. Clair Road near Greenfield is named for him. Perhaps St. Clair Avenue that runs south of the main library and north of Huntsville Hospital is named for these St. Clairs.

Or maybe the avenue is named for Arthur St. Clair. He fought during the Revolution, was with General Washington at Valley Forge, served as a president of the Continental Congress, and was Governor of the Northwest Territory. Alabama's St. Clair County is named for him.

Or perhaps it was just a name the street department came up with.

STEELE STREET. It is a block east of Lincoln Street in the Old Town Historic District, and it honors George Gilliam Steele, considered the premier architect of his time in Huntsville. Steele was born in Virginia and arrived in Huntsville around 1818. His architectural skills were self-taught. First such project was to build his home in 1824 – it still stands at 519 Randolph Avenue. Also standing are eight antebellum homes he was responsible for, plus the portico of the Pope mansion and the First National Bank Building on West Side Square. Steele died in 1855.

WEATHERLY ROAD. Peter Weatherly, from Berwickshire, Scotland, purchased land in 1853 just south of the road that bears the Weatherly name and east beyond what is now Bailey Cove Road. He built a log cabin and began farming. Peter died in 1872 and his lands passed to his great nephew, also named Peter. This Peter and his wife, Sarah Bache Weatherly, also farmed the lands successfully. They had nine children. Over time Weatherly farm lands were sold to developers, the last in 1986.

WHITESBURG DRIVE. James White owned iron works and salt factories in East Tennessee. He traded salt for land and thus owned a lot of land on both sides of the Tennessee River. Salt was in demand for a variety of uses, including preservation of meats, and White eventually established a monopoly for salt - so much so that he became known as "Salt" White. By 1825, the Ditto's Landing area had become known as Whitesburg. The Whitesburg community that grew up in the area was burned and destroyed by Union forces during the Civil War and never revived.

Whitesburg Drive, between Huntsville and the Tennessee River, opened in 1834 as a toll road. It operated that way until 1895 when a state commission outlawed the charges.

6. More Huntsville Streets

WYNN DRIVE. This is a major street through Cummings Research Park and running north to Oakwood University.

Virginians John and Polly Wynne (and there are various spellings of Wynn) settled near South Pittsburgh, Tennessee. From there, grandchildren and great grandchildren "moved all over northern Alabama and into other states. Huntsville has its share of early Wynn families and even has a Wynn Drive named for one of them." That was John P. Rankin writing about the Wynn family for *The Heritage of Madison County.*

7. IN AND AROUND MADISON

The first known settler in what is now the city of Madison was John Cartwright, who arrived in 1818. However the town of Madison wasn't established, until 1857 when it became a station on the Memphis and Charleston Railroad and was known as Madison Station. The local Historic District and the Historical Preservation Society today use that name.

James Clemens is considered the founder of Madison. He was born in Pennsylvania and showed up in Huntsville in 1812. It is his original home that now stands in Huntsville at the intersection of Pratt Avenue and Meridian Street.

In 1854 Clemens bought lands halfway between Decatur and Huntsville. It was his plan to establish a village around the depot that had been built by the then-new Memphis and Charleston Railroad. He laid out town lots fronting on the railroad (hence the name Front Street). On Front Street a house was built for the station agent, Thomas J. Clay. The depot was across the tracks. There were 55 lots in all for sale to potential merchants and residents. First buyers in 1857 were George Washington Martin and Thomas J. Clay.

Clemens died in 1860 at age 83. He had sold 15 of the 55 lots by that time.

Madison was incorporated in 1869. A historical marker lists its first officials: William R. Johnston, mayor, and aldermen William B. Dunn, then the depot agent; Thomas J. Clay, the first postmaster; George W. Martin, the town's first merchant; James H. Bibb, a planter; and the town doctor, Dr. George R. Sullivan.

Madison didn't begin to grow to its present size until after activities at Redstone Arsenal expanded. In 1955, Madison was only one-half square mile in total size. In 1956 its first subdivision began to be developed. And by 1957, the city was forced to buy its first police car. Today Madison's population is shown to be over 42,000.

BALCH ROAD. This is a north-south road on the west side of Madison.

Joseph A. Balch, Jr., ran the grocery store on Main Street. In the early 1950s as the town began to expand, he served on the city commission and its industrial development board. Woodrow Alden Balch was from Monrovia, a farmer, and county commissioner for a dozen years. Contrary to what many people told me, the road is not named for either.

Hezekiah Balch - apparently the first Balch in the area - was born in Sparta, Tennessee, in 1811, and moved to Madison County about 1830, where he operated a grist mill on Indian Creek. A grandson, Jesse Burton Balch, born in 1878, eventually married Gertrude Clutts. Jesse was apparently the only one of his generation to stay all his life on the original plot of land, and it is for him that the road is named.

In writing about the Gooch family for *The Heritage of Madison County*, Barbara Gooch Ciliax wrote "Gooch Lane joins Balch Road at the west end. Balch Road was named for Jesse Balch, who later became Richard's father-in-law." Richard Gooch married Ada Mable Balch in 1924.

BUTTERMILK ALLEY. This narrow one-block lane runs from Front Street to Arnett Street. Its place on Front Street is just across the railroad tracks from where the old station stood. It got its name from Mrs. William Humphrey, whose home was on its corner, giving buttermilk and bread to the hobos who rode the trains during the Great Depression years of the 1930s. The city formally recognized the name in 1986 by putting up an official street sign.

DUBLIN MEMORIAL PARK. In 1995, Mamie Dublin Smith donated 60 acres to the City of Madison - if they would use it for recreation purposes and if they would name it after two of her family members. Two years later the park opened. It sports a gym, swimming pool, soccer fields, tennis courts, pavilions, and ball fields in a nice landscaped setting off Old Madison Pike. And as Mrs. Smith specified, it is named for Clyde Harris Dublin and Mary Caldwell Dublin.

GOOCH LANE. Roland Gooch bought land near Madison in 1818, and moved his wife Elizabeth and their five children here from Virginia. They had three more children in Madison, and there are many Gooch family members in the area. Much later, Matt Roland Gooch, a grandchild, married Mary Pike. They lived in what is now the northwest part of Madison on Old Athens Pike, the name of which was changed to Gooch Lane after their son Richard Matson Gooch, who worked for the state highway department for 19 years.

HUGHES ROAD. In recent years, this road has become the main north-south street of Madison. It is named for the Hughes family, most notable of whom is probably G. Walton Hughes. For over 50 years he was Madison's only druggist. Walton was the eldest son of Madison settler John A. Hughes and his wife Laura Vaughn Hughes. The family did successful farming on over 400 acres along this road.

In 1922 Walton had completed requirements for pharmacy, married Sarah Parham, and took a job in Huntsville. It was about 1924 when he bought the Burton & Wise Drug Store in Madison, across from the railroad depot. He remained there for the next 50 years. He was known as "Doc" to many of his customers. He was always active in community affairs and served as mayor from 1944 to 1949.

NANCE ROAD. In 1928 Mrs. Annie Elizabeth Nance Cain was killed when her car was hit by a fast-moving freight train. The north-south road that crosses the railroad where she was killed bears her name.

PALMER ROAD. Oziah Palmer was a soldier with the Ohio Volunteers who liked the area and returned to Madison after the Civil War to buy 80 acres. In 1870 his brother Samuel and his wife Ginny followed him and purchased the land from him. They had ten children, among them Roy and Octavia, born in 1874 and 1876. In 1900, Roy added 122 more acres to the farm. He was a successful farmer and was active in community affairs. Roy died in 1962, Octavia in 1965.

Palmer Road and the extensive Palmer Park, which is located at their home site, take their names from this family.

PENSION ROW. A few blocks west of downtown is a street, indeed an old community, known by this name. It was one of the first black communities in Madison, and the only one remaining. It got its name after the Civil War because its residents were living off federal pensions they received for fighting for the Union.

RAINBOW MOUNTAIN. This little mountain in Madison lies between Slaughter and Hughes Roads, just north of Old Madison Pike. There's a Rainbow Drive and some Rainbow subdivisions - and they shouldn't be "Rainbows" at all. The property was owned by original settler Elisha Rainbolt and his wife Phyllis (which he spelled Fillas). His name came from a Dutch ancestor and was originally spelled Reinboldt. Pronounce that name, and you can see why early settlers misunderstood it and called it Rainbow.

SLAUGHTER ROAD. There's a courthouse record of a John Slaughter leaving land via a will to James Slaughter in 1812, and other records soon thereafter involving John, James, William, Thomas, and Samuel Slaughter. So these were all quite early area settlers. But the story I have about the road is as follows:

Virginian Robert Lanford came to Huntsville in 1809. He was a wealthy planter who bought 2,500 acres west of Huntsville. His son, William, built his home in the area, on Madison Pike near Indian Creek. William had three children, and one of his daughters, Mary Elizabeth, married Dr. John Robert Slaughter. When William was old, Mary and John came to live with him. Dr. Slaughter practiced medicine from an office built on the property. Slaughter Road runs north and south at the east edge of Madison and along Indian Creek, and the road takes its name from Dr. Slaughter.

SULLIVAN STREET. Where Wall-Triana Road goes through Madison, it changes its name to Sullivan Street, named for the city's first doctor, G. R. Sullivan. Dr. Sullivan also set up the first drug store in Madison, in 1871.

8. BUILDINGS

Many buildings in the city and county are named and known for their owners. There are also lots of buildings - a pretty broad term – mentioned in Chapters 12 through 15 of this book. Here are a few, each of which has an intriguing story behind its name.

BELK HUDSON LOFTS. The building at the corner of Washington Street and Holmes Avenue was built in 1930 to house Fowler's Department Store. Fowler's went bankrupt in 1938, and in 1940 Belk Hudson purchased the building where it operated as a department store until the 1980s. After 2010, when the building was renovated and converted to loft apartments, developers decided to keep the now-historic Belk Hudson name.

BLOUNT HOSPITALITY HOUSE. The house opened in 1980 as The Hospital Hospitality House of Huntsville, and was the first such house in Alabama. The present facility, on Madison Street two blocks north of Huntsville Hospital, is actually a complex of ten units which provide lodging and support for out-of-town relatives of patients in the city's hospitals – a sort of home away from home for families in need. The home was completed in 1988, and the name was changed to honor its original executive director Bernice Blount who served 25 years as director. Mrs. Blount retired in 2006.

C.F. BOST BUILDING. This building is on Jefferson Street, downtown, across from the parking garage and a couple doors south of the W.T. Hutchens Building. At its top is a block inscribed "C.F. Bost, 1921." Chalmers F. Bost was a contractor and builder in Huntsville from the 1890s to the late 1930s.

CHARLES H. STONE AGRICULTURAL CENTER. Charles Stone attended school in Huntsville and at Auburn

University. In 1956 he joined his father Roy Stone, long-time chairman of the Madison County Commission, in dairy farming near Gurley. He was recognized as Outstanding Young Farmer in America, and became involved in government. He was elected to the Commission from District 2 in 1976, and re-elected in 1980 and 1984. In 1986, Charles died of cancer at age 51.

This Madison County building - on Cook Street across from the Farmers Market - was built the year Charles died. It houses the County Extension Service, Sales Tax office, Planning and Economic Development organization, and Board of Registrars.

ELBERT H. PARSONS PUBLIC LAW LIBRARY. One of the most conspicuous names on Courthouse Square isn't really that of a building, but it's that of Madison County's Elbert H. Parsons Public Law Library. The library was moved from the courthouse about 1973, across the street to East Side Square where J.C. Penney did business from 1934 to 1965. The building itself was built in 1913 for the May and Cooney Dry Goods Company, which operated until 1931, when it went bankrupt in the Great Depression.

Parsons was born on Hobbs Island in 1908, obtained a law degree from the University of Alabama at age 19, and moved to West Side Square in 1931. In 1933 he was appointed registrar of chancery court, then in 1945 was appointed circuit judge. He had a stern demeanor in court, yet was known as knowledgeable and fair. He was never opposed in his bids for re-election. Judge Parsons died in 1968.

FLOYD E. "TUT" FANN STATE VETERANS HOME. Floyd E. "Tut" Fann was a lifelong resident of Madison County. He served in the military during World War II, seeing action at the Battle of the Bulge where he was wounded and for which he received the Purple Heart. Fann spent almost twenty years on the Alabama Board of Veteran Affairs, and was state commander of the American Legion and a president of the Military Heritage Commission and Hall of Heroes. Locally Fann was instrumental in having the tombstones of Confederate veterans in Maple Hill Cemetery replaced with those now neatly in place, and in seeing that a memorial was erected in Brahan Spring Park for veterans of World War I. He worked hard for many years to have a state veterans home established in Huntsville. Fann died in 1992. The home on Meridian Street that bears his name was opened and dedicated to him in 1995.

FORENSIC SCIENCES BUILDING. In 1935 long before forensic science became a present-day staple of television crime shows, the Alabama Department of Toxicology and Criminal Investigation was established with headquarters at Auburn University. Today its name is Department of Forensic Sciences. Its local building is on Acadia Circle, a street most people don't travel, a block north of the Farmers Market. The Huntsville laboratory is known as the Wheeler-Pruitt Forensic Science Laboratory, dedicated to those two men in 2001.

Brent Allen Wheeler obtained B.S. and M.S. degrees from Auburn. He began service with the department in Huntsville in 1971. He became laboratory director in Huntsville in 1975 and served in that capacity for 25 years. He was an expert in firearm and tool mark identification. In 2000 he moved to Opelika when he was appointed deputy director of the Headquarters Lab at Auburn. He retired in 2006. Wheeler died in 2012.

Vann Pruitt, Jr. obtained his B.S. degree from Auburn in 1953. He was the first laboratory director in Huntsville from 1964 to 1975. Afterwards he was deputy director of the department until his retirement in 1988 after 35 years of service. He was known as a brilliant teacher and a rock-solid witness whose court testimony was never impeached. He, like Wheeler, died in 2012.

8. Buildings

FORT JACKSON M. BALCH. After the National Guard Armory on Dallas Street burned down, a site at Airport Road and Leeman Ferry Road was chosen. The armory building was completed in 1971 but had no name. When Col. Balch died in 1980, National Guard members requested it be named for him.

Jackson Balch was born in Nova Scotia, Canada, son of Henry and Josephine Balch of Huntsville. In 1941 he enlisted in the infantry, served through World War II (at one time as aide to General MacArthur), and in 1946 left active duty as a lieutenant colonel. In 1951 he joined the Alabama National Guard and commanded the 279th Anti-Aircraft Artillery Battalion. He has been credited with making the Alabama National Guard largest in the nation and moving its headquarters to North Alabama.

Balch moved on to joint NASA on Wernher von Braun's staff He took over as director of NASA's Mississippi Test Operations facility, later named the Stennis Space Center, and served as director there from 1965 to 1974, and as director of the National Space Technology Laboratory from 1974 to 1976.

HALSEY GROCERY. The 1904 Halsey Building on Jefferson Street still contains the Halsey grocery business (now known as Halsey Foodservice). Charles Halsey and his brother Leroy started their business nearby in 1879.

James Record has written that a John Halsey had a chair-manufacturing business in Huntsville in 1817 a block from this building, and that would make this the oldest continuous business in the city or county.

HARRISON BROTHERS HARDWARE STORE. This store, on South Side Square, is the oldest operating hardware store in the state. Harrison Brothers Hardware began in 1879 in Smithville, Tennessee, by the local brothers' uncles. It was founded in Huntsville in the same year by nephews James and

Daniel Harrison as a tobacco store on Jefferson Street. It moved to this location in 1897, expanded next door in 1902, and, over the years, had its stock increased to include crockery, furniture, appliances, and finally hardware. Younger brother Robert, and later his sons Daniel and John, ran the store until 1983, when John, last of the brothers, died. In 1984 the family sold the store to the Historic Huntsville Foundation, which has preserved and operated it since then.

*(A **little advertisement:** Because it is operated by the Historic Huntsville Foundation, Harrison Brothers Hardware is the place to go for additional copies of this and other local history books. This book is also available at area gift shops and at Shaver's Bookstore, on the second floor of the Railroad Station Antique Mall at 315 N. Jefferson Street. John Shaver once said that, in his over 40 years of book selling, he sold more copies of* Why Is It Named That? *than any other book.)*

HAROLD H. POTTS CENTER. In 2009, the Huntsville-Madison County 911 Center on the corner of Oakwood Avenue and John Road was given this new name. Potts had been chairman of the center's Board of Commissioners since 1993. He oversaw the building of the complex in 1997. He has been called Madison County's 9-1-1 Pioneer.

The Center is the call-taking and radio dispatch facility for all Huntsville and Madison County public safety agencies. It is the largest in Alabama. There are 36 call taker/dispatch positions. In 2013, for example, they answered over 240,000 calls.

HARVIE JONES BUILDING. Harvie P. Jones was born in Huntsville in 1930. He grew up in New Market, graduated from high school there, went to Georgia Institute of Technology where he earned B.S. and B.Arch degrees. He returned to Huntsville, worked as a designer for G.W. Jones & Sons, joined W.R. Dickson, Architect. He became a partner in 1964. In 1967 he and

8. Buildings

Billy Herrin formed Jones & Herrin Architects/Interior Design. Jones would remain with the firm until his death in 1998.

Jones' contributions to historic preservation are enormous. Diane Ellis, former executive director of the Historic Huntsville Foundation, has written, "Perhaps more than any other person, he influenced the appearance of the city. Without Harvie there might have been no historic downtown business district. No Twickenham Historic District. No Old Town Historic District. ... No Alabama Constitution Village. No historic passenger depot."

Jones served on many professional and civic boards. He authored numerous articles on historic architecture and preservation. He worked on over 600 preservation projects.

The Historic Huntsville Foundation is known for operating Harrison Brothers store on South Side Square, but HHF also bought the building next to it at the corner of Franklin Street. In 2001 HHF dedicated the building to Harvie Jones.

HENDERSON NATIONAL BANK. On Jefferson Street and built in its present form in 1948, it is the only Art Moderne style building in downtown Huntsville. Outer walls are built of white stone, the front doorway and base of green stone.

Fox Henderson grew up in Troy, Alabama. In 1881 he and his brother Clem purchased the Pike County Bank and in the 1880s followed with hardware, fertilizer, and chemical businesses. In 1900 he was one of the largest landowners in Troy. By 1911, he was president or vice president of seven banks in Alabama including the one in Huntsville. Fox Henderson died in 1918.

HISTORIC HUNTSVILLE DEPOT. Located on Church Street, this three-story railroad depot is one of the oldest in the country. It was constructed in 1860 and served as the eastern division headquarters of the Memphis and Charleston Railroad.

During the Civil War, it was occupied by Union forces and used as a prison for Confederate soldiers. In 1898 it was taken over by Norfolk Southern Railway. Southern's passenger trains ran through Huntsville until 1968. In 1971, the city obtained the depot and turned it into a museum, now one of the city's major attractions. Nearby are a train turntable, locomotive, items of rolling stock, and a roundhouse used for social events.

Eunice's Country Kitchen. It was the place for a good Southern breakfast, and a favorite of state-wide and local politicians who often frequented Eunice's round "liar's" table. "Aunt" Eunice was listed in the Congressional Record, her biscuits were named the official biscuit of Alabama, and she was honored by dozens of organizations. Eunice Isabell Jenkins Merrell ran the restaurant on Andrew Jackson Way in the Five Points area for 52 years. Eunice died in 2004 and after the original building was torn down in 2007, the city relocated restaurant contents to the odd-looking maroon-colored building in the middle of the Huntsville Depot grounds.

HOUSING AUTHORITY BUILDINGS. The Huntsville Housing Authority (HHA), formed in 1941, operates low-cost housing projects at several locations in the city. Most are named for people.

Butler Terrace. These homes along Governors Drive are HHA's oldest property. They began in 1951 when Huntsville started to clear some of its slum areas. They are named for educator Samuel Riley Butler who had just died in 1947.

Butler was born in Poplar Ridge, Alabama, in 1868. He graduated from Winchester Normal College in 1890. He moved to Huntsville to teach and spent 40 years in local schools, as superintendent of public schools (1893-1906), principal of the private State School of Huntsville (1906-08), principal and owner of his own Butler School (1908-14), and county superintendent of public education (1905-31).

Johnson Towers. These high-rise apartments are on Seminole Drive just off Governors Drive. They were opened in 1964 and are named for Herbert Johnson, one of the original HHA commissioners in 1941.

Johnson was born in Water Valley, Mississippi, and came to Huntsville in 1910 as the first director of the then-new YMCA (Young Men's Christian Association). In 1916, he and George Mahoney established the Johnson & Mahoney clothing store, which operated well over 50 years. In 1966, Johnson was named "Huntsville's Outstanding Citizen" by the Chamber of Commerce. He died in 1967, still serving as an HHA commissioner at that time.

Lincoln Park. This collection of homes is several blocks west of where Lincoln Mill stood and takes its name from the mill.

L.R. Patton Apartments on Seminole Drive are named for Leander R. Patton, a member of the HHA board.

Patton was born in Perry County and grew up in Marion. After high school he served four years in the U.S. Army. He obtained his B.S. degree from Alabama A&M University in 1946 and a year later joined A&M as veterans coordinator. He later served as financial secretary and business-manager treasurer. In 1971 he became vice-president for business and finance. That same year the Alabama Legislature named the school's administration building the L.R. Patton Building. Patton retired in 1985 after 40 years of service, after which A&M awarded him an honorary Doctor of Laws degree. Patton died in 1989.

Mayor Joe Davis appointed Patton to the HHA board of commissioners in 1977. Patton was its first black member.

8. Buildings

Oscar Mason Community Center. William Oscar Mason was born in Huntsville in 1901. He was an original 1941 member of HHA and served as chairman from 1955 to 1972. He also served as a member of the Hospital, Public Library, and County Building Authorities. These were responsible for the design and construction of the Madison County Courthouse, Huntsville City Hall, new wing of Huntsville Hospital, and main library. Mason still found time to be on the boards of directors of many civic organizations as well. He died in 1972. The center and its branch library that bear his name are on Mason Court, off West Holmes Avenue, next to Sparkman Homes. The center was dedicated to him in 1993.

Searcy Homes. These single-family dwellings are on Monroe Street on the north edge of downtown. They are named for Huntsville Mayor R.B. "Speck" Searcy.

Searcy was born in Huntsville, became mayor just when the Germans were arriving to work at Redstone Arsenal and the city was about to explode in population and needed services. Searcy was mayor from 1952 to 1964, and is credited with changing Huntsville from a cotton town into a space age metropolis. During those dozen years, city size (i.e., land area) doubled to become the second largest in Alabama, and downtown urban renewal was begun - especially in the area from Memorial Parkway to the Big Spring.

A piece of trivia: When Herbert Johnson (see above) became YMCA director, young Searcy was in his first class. The two were good friends. They died on the same day, December 22, 1967.

Sparkman Homes. The group of homes served by the Oscar Mason Community Center and just off of Holmes Avenue is named for former Senator John J. Sparkman. (See 10. Sparkman High School for his story.)

79

8. Buildings

Todd Towers. This high-rise building at the north end of Greene Street downtown is named for Ashford Todd. He was another of the original 1941 commissioners on the HHA, and served until 1968.

Todd was born in Limestone County, and moved to Huntsville in 1921 to join the W.R. Rison Bank, where he worked until it consolidated with the First National Bank in 1948. For a few years he worked as a consultant on Redstone Arsenal, then in 1952 won election as probate judge. He served as judge for 18 years, retiring in 1970. Todd died in 1973.

HUNTSVILLE HOSPITAL. The hospital has two of its buildings named for people. The main hospital building itself is not named for a person. Still some of its many benefactors are recognized by plaques, name plates, and pictures in its corridors.

Back of the first floor's main lobby, there is a rotunda in which are paintings that tell hospital history, for example the story of Mollie Teal, the city's well known madam of a house of prostitution, who died in 1899 and willed her house to the city for school or hospital use. The city chose hospital, and the Huntsville Infirmary moved to the house in 1904 and stayed until 1926. In 1926, city leaders Carl Grote and Harry Rhett headed a drive for a new hospital. Near the elevators that are in the main lobby and serve the newest hospital wing are two portraits and a plaque that says "dedicated to Dr. Carl A. Grote, Sr., and Dr. Carl A. Grote, Jr., for their lifelong commitment to patient care, for their leadership and support of the institution, and for their dedicated service to this commitment." Near the elevators in the older wing is a portrait of "Harry Moore Rhett, 1873-1948, [who] donated the land for Huntsville Hospital, 1925."

Blackwell Medical Tower. It stands to the west, across Gallatin Street. A plaque in its lobby states that it is "named for T. Alvin Blackwell, Huntsville Hospital Board of Directors, 1961-1993."

Blackwell was born in the Hurricane Creek area, graduated from Riverton High School, served in the Navy in World War II, and got his degree in business from the University of Alabama. He went to work for G.W. Jones & Company, but soon started his own real estate business. He served in - indeed chaired - many civic endeavors, from heart and cancer drives, to being president of the Huntsville Industrial Expansion Committee. In 1961 Blackwell was named to the governing body of Huntsville Hospital, where he served as president for over 25 years. It was under his leadership that the hospital grew to its present capacity that serves north Alabama and south-central Tennessee.

Dowdle Center. This stand-alone building is at the corner of Governors Drive and Gallatin Street. It is home to the hospital's Corporate University and is named for Dr. Joseph C. Dowdle who was a member of the city's Health Care Authority from 1981 until his death in 2004. The Dowdle Center building was dedicated to him in 2005.

Dr. Dowdle got degrees from Auburn, then his Ph.D. from North Carolina State. In the 1960s he was on the faculty of the UAH electrical engineering department and in the 1970s became vice president for administration. He even served as UAH CEO in 1976-1977. But it was his 23 years of service with the Health Care Authority that saw unprecedented growth for the hospital and for which his leadership and direction were vital.

HUNTSVILLE MUSEUM OF ART. The museum's current facility on Church Street opened in 1998. It provided 15,000 square feet of exhibit space. By 2006 HMA had added its Plaza in the Park, providing eating and shopping areas and expanding the building to 52,000 square feet. Then in 2007, the museum began a further expansion and conducted one of the largest fundraising efforts the city had seen. Over 170 donors responded, and many of the museum's galleries now are named for significant contributors. Listing and describing them all is beyond the scope of this book. Here, though, is a major one:

Davidson Center for the Arts. As a result of the above fundraising effort, this additional wing to the museum opened in 2010, and is named after Dorothy and Dr. Julian Davidson whose $2 million was the largest contribution and formed a basis for the expansion. There is a circular driveway off Williams Avenue that provides a more convenient entrance, especially for groups, there are seven new galleries, and, as a key feature, there is a stage integrated into the building that is now home for the city's popular summertime concerts and movies in Big Spring Park.

I. SCHIFFMAN BUILDING. On East Side Square, this building is best known as the birthplace of actress Tallulah Bankhead. But it was just a store when it was originally put up in 1840. The Romanesque facade was added in 1895. Isaac Schiffman, for whom the building is now named, bought it in 1905 and used it as headquarters for his land holdings and investments. In 1906 he was joined by his son-in-law, Lawrence Goldsmith. (See 15. Goldsmith-Schiffman Field.) The Schiffman real estate management business continues there today.

LINCOLN MILL OFFICE CAMPUS. In 1918 William Lincoln Barrell of Lowell, Massachusetts, bought the Abington Mill, vastly expanded it, and renamed it Lincoln Mill. A new mill building was constructed in 1923-24, followed by a 1927 expansion that included Mill No. 3. About a year later a store, community center, and school were added. The area around all this, known as Lincoln Village, grew too. Tents made from Lincoln Mill canvas sheltered Army units in World War II and the Korean War. But the mill stopped operation in the 1950s. In 1958 a group of civic leaders bought the property, converted it into offices, and it became home to the city's new missile businesses, such as Brown Engineering and part of the Army

8. Buildings

Ballistic Missile Agency. In 1980 the oldest mill buildings along Oakwood Avenue were destroyed by fire, leaving only the dye house and the big Mill No. 3 office building. In 2007 Dr. James Byrne and his business partner Wayne Sisco bought the buildings and began their most recent renovation. Today, at 1300 Meridian Street, the Mill No. 3 building is home to over a dozen innovative companies.

South of the campus area some of the original mill village houses and the 1929 Lincoln School still exist. The building that housed the company store is being renovated.

LOMBARDO BUILDING. At the corner of Monroe and Jefferson Streets, this building is clearly marked at the top with "Lombardo 1922." In the 1890s, Peter Lombardo established a grocery business in Huntsville that lasted over 40 years. The Lombardo Wholesale Grocery Company operated out of this building, now the site of an antique mall and local bookstore.

LOWE MILL. In 1900 the Lowe Manufacturing Company was incorporated in Huntsville, and its cotton mill became operational in 1901 in what is now West Huntsville. The mill was named for Arthur M. Lowe of Fitchburg, Massachusetts, who held controlling interest until he sold out in 1907. The mill operated under various owners and management until 1937 when it was sold to Walter Laxson who used it as a cotton warehouse. In 1946 General Shoe Company began to manufacture shoes in the mill. It changed its name to Genesco in 1959, and in the 1960s during the Vietnam War produced the majority of combat boots for U.S. soldiers. The company closed operations in 1978.

In 2001 Lowe Mill was purchased by Jim Hudson, founder of HudsonAlpha Institute for Biotechnology. Over fifteen years, Hudson has turned the mill buildings into the nation's largest privately owned "ARTS and Entertainment" facility. At 2211 Seminole Drive, it is home to 140 public studios, 200 working artists, half-dozen fine-art galleries, a multi-use theatre and other performance venues.

MASON FURNITURE BUILDING. Downtown at 115 Clinton Avenue, this building was built in the 1920s by the owners of Mason Furniture with the intent to lease it to other tenants. Sears Roebuck began leasing it in 1929 when a mezzanine was added, but Sears left at the start of the Depression, and Mason Furniture moved into its own store and operated there until 1977. Despite many tenants over the years, the words Mason Furniture are still in the tile floor to greet entering visitors, and the mezzanine is still in use. Today the building is occupied by U.G. White Mercantile, a business from nearby Athens that was started there in 1917. (By the way, the U.G. stands for Ulysses Grant.)

MERRIMACK HALL. The Merrimack Manufacturing Company of Lowell, Massachusetts, built its mills here, on the east side of Triana Boulevard, between 1899 and 1903. It was the largest of all the Huntsville textile mills. Its name came from the river on which its New England facility was located. The mill's company store and village houses were on the west side of Triana Boulevard. In 1920, the company store, Merrimack Hall, was enlarged. When it opened it contained a gym, community rooms, company store and drug store, café, barbershop, and meat market. The hall served as a center point of activity for the mill village around it. After World War II, the company was sold to M. Lowenstein and Company which further expanded the hall – at one time it included four bowling lanes and a boxing ring. In 1989 mill operation ended, after almost a hundred years. In 1992, the city demolished the mill, turning the area into a series of soccer fields and naming it Merrimack Park. But the hall, across the street, remained.

In 2006 Debra and Alan Jenkins purchased the hall and put in $2.5 million of renovations. The facility, now called the Merrimack Hall Performing Arts Center, has a 300-seat auditorium, a large dance studio, and community spaces. The Jenkins family provides year-around arts education and social and cultural opportunities to children, teens, and adults with intellectual and physical disabilities.

ROBERT "BUD" CRAMER, JR., NATIONAL CHILDREN'S ADVOCACY CENTER. "Bud" Cramer was born and raised in Huntsville. In 1972 he earned his law degree from the University of Alabama. For ten years he was Madison County's district attorney. He became aware of the trauma that child victims experienced when they had to be interviewed repeatedly in different locations by law enforcement, child protective services, prosecution, mental health, medical, educational and other well-meaning groups responding to child abuse. In 1985 he established the first children's advocacy center to bring such agencies together and stress their cooperation.

In 1991, Cramer was elected to the House of Representatives where he represented Alabama's Fifth Congressional District for nine terms before his retirement in 2008. He saw his advocacy program enacted into law. The center here serves as a model for what is collectively known as the National Children's Alliance and which today boasts 950 centers in the U.S. and 25 foreign countries. In 2003 the local center moved into the national facility on Pratt Avenue that bears Cramer's name.

RUSSEL ERSKINE APARTMENTS. A best-known landmark in Huntsville for over 50 years, the former Russel Erskine Hotel is now an apartment building.

Albert Russel Erskine was born in Huntsville in 1871. He was named for Revolutionary War ancestor, Albert Russel. He dropped out of school when he was 15, worked as an office boy, moved to St. Louis, soon was chief auditor for American Cotton Company in charge of 300 cotton gins. By 1911 Erskine was vice president of the Underwood Typewriter Company. That same year he joined Studebaker Corporation in South Bend, Indiana, and by 1915 became its president. It was Erskine that moved Studebaker from manufacturing horse drawn carriages to automobiles and international renown.

In 1925 a group of Huntsville businessmen started to build the Wheeler Hotel (to be named for General Joe Wheeler) (see 15. Wheeler National Wildlife Refuge), to be the city's 12-story show place. They ran out of money and turned to former resident Erskine, who had become a millionaire. Erskine agreed to put up the remaining money on the condition that the hotel bear his name. The hotel opened in 1930. Its Russel Erskine Hotel sign could be seen for miles.

By 1933 the Great Depression had hit America, Studebaker had gone into receivership, and at 63, Erskine was in failing health. That July, Erskine shot himself. The South Bend papers quoted his note: "Nervous System Shattered I Cannot Go On." Erskine was brought back to Huntsville and entombed in the family mausoleum in Maple Hill Cemetery.

S.H. KRESS BUILDING. On Washington Street there is an S.H. Kress Building, remains of the five-and-ten-cent store chain. The chain was begun in 1896 in Memphis by Samuel Henry Kress. The store in Huntsville opened in 1905. There was a fire, and the store was rebuilt in 1930. On the front is the S.H. Kress name in stone; the style of the facade is art deco. Kress used an in-house staff of architects that gave his stores a consistent exterior design that other stores lacked. Art experts have noted that the Kress chain "more than any other, was responsible for bringing Art Deco to Main Street."

In 1924 Kress set up a foundation, devoted his life to art collecting, and bought and gave away millions of dollars of art pieces. He became president and trustee of the National Gallery of Art in Washington. Kress died in 1955. The chain of stores went out of business in 1981. The local store at this writing is occupied by a nightclub.

TERRY-HUTCHENS BUILDING. This building stands on the northwest corner of Jefferson Street and Clinton Avenue. (Its main entrance is at 115 Clinton Avenue.) It was designed by B.F. Hunt of Chattanooga in Gothic Revival style and built in 1925. At seven stories, it was the city's first sky scraper. It opened as the State National Bank Building. The two families for whom the building is known bought it in the 1940s. A plaque on the building lists I.M. Terry, M.M. Hutchens, W.C. Hutchens, and V.F. Hutchens, with a date of 1944.

The Terrys were merchants whose store was on South Side Square from 1897 until well after World War II. It was famous for its signs, "Great Is The Power of Cash" and "T.T. Terry." Founder of Terry's Store was Thomas Tyler Terry. Three brothers were also involved, and in 1936 Jim Terry, a nephew, took over. When he died in 1941, his son, Ira M. Terry, became proprietor. Ira is the Terry of the Terry-Hutchens Building.

At present, the Terry-Hutchens Building has been converted into business offices, a coffee shop, and apartments. (For information about the Hutchens, see the W.T. Hutchens Building later in this chapter.)

THOMAS W. DAVIDSON SENIOR CENTER. In 2002, the Huntsville-Madison County Senior Center on Drake Avenue was renamed in memory of Thomas W. Davidson, Sr. He was the safety manager at Redstone Arsenal for over twenty years and had served on the Center's board of directors for over a dozen years, four times as its president. Davidson also helped plan and design the current facility, and played a significant role in obtaining financing for it.

TIMES BUILDING at Holmes Avenue and Greene Street, was built in 1930 by Emory Pierce to house *The Huntsville Daily Times* newspaper. After the builder of the Russel Erskine Hotel announced it would be twelve stories high, Pierce added a twelfth story not in his original plans to make sure the Times Building would be the tallest in the city - and it was the tallest building in the city for most of the 20th century.

U.S. SPACE AND ROCKET CENTER. Sometimes called "Earth's largest space museum" the center showcases rockets, achievements, and artifacts of the U.S. space program. There are over 1,500 permanent items on display encompassing efforts from original attempts to put a man in space through the lunar landings. Exhibits include the Pathfinder space shuttle, Skylab, and lunar landing module, as well as the standing Saturn V rocket that can be seen not only from adjacent I-565 but from locations throughout the city. The center is also home of Space Camp. Most important perhaps are the rockets that made U.S. space travel possible and gave Huntsville its name of Rocket City.

Davidson Center for Space Exploration. This is the newest building added to the U.S. Space and Rocket Center. It is named for Dr. Julian Davidson, founder of Davidson Technologies. He and his wife Dorothy donated $2 million toward the building that now bears his name, a 68,000 square foot affair that houses one of the three Saturn V vehicles still in existence. Dr. Davidson was a graduate of Auburn University and was an early pioneer in U.S. space, missile, and missile defense programs. He was the first director of the Advanced Ballistic Missile Defense Agency at Redstone Arsenal in the late 1960s. His career spanned 60 years. Davidson died in 2013.

U.S. VETERANS MEMORIAL MUSEUM. A rather nondescript building just off Airport Road houses this museum, operated by the nonprofit Alabama Center of Military History.

8. Buildings

There are displays and memorabilia dating back to the Revolutionary War, but with the emphasis on World War I and subsequent conflicts. Some items are considered rare. There are also special displays pertaining to North Alabama residents who served in the military.

The city named the building the **Paul Bolden Military Museum,** although his name is no longer used in the museum's publicity. (See 3. Paul Luther Bolden Memorial Highway.)

VON BRAUN CENTER. During the 1960s numerous civic and arts groups combined with city officials to try to get some sort of theater/museum/convention building. In 1975 their dream was realized with the opening of the Von Braun Center. It contains a small theater, large concert hall, sports arena, and exhibition and convention halls. It is named for Huntsville's most widely known citizen, Wernher von Braun. Von Braun may be known to outsiders as a foremost rocket scientist from another country. But he was also a man who took time to be part of the Huntsville community, and participated in and helped promote numerous civic and arts endeavors.

Von Braun was born in Germany in 1912. He held a bachelor's degree from the Berlin Institute of Technology and a doctor's degree in physics from the University of Berlin. He received a grant from the German Ordnance Department, and a rocket group was organized at Peenemunde in 1937. They developed a ballistic missile eventually designated the V-2 (V for vengeance) and used against Great Britain in World War II. At the end of the war, von Braun and his top engineers surrendered to the U.S. Army and were offered the opportunity to continue their work, first in Texas, then at Redstone Arsenal.

Under von Braun's direction, the Army produced the Redstone rocket and Jupiter intermediate range ballistic missile. In 1958 a modified Redstone (the Jupiter C) put the first U.S. satellite into orbit. In 1960, the newly formed National Aeronautics and Space Administration took over von Braun's team and created the Marshall Space Flight Center, separate from Army facilities but still at Redstone Arsenal. Von Braun continued development of larger rockets, including the Saturn I, the IB used for the Apollo program, and the Saturn V, which enabled man to go to the moon.

In 1970, von Braun moved to Washington to become NASA's Deputy Associate Administrator for Planning. In 1972 he joined private industry as vice-president of Fairchild Industries. Fairchild had gotten into the satellite business, and von Braun - ahead of his time as usual - envisioned development of satellites for mapping, navigation, weather prediction, and worldwide communications. Von Braun died in 1977.

Mark C. Smith Concert Hall. In 2008, a $3 million gift from the family of Mark Smith was used to replace seats, add luxury suites, create a center aisle, improve restrooms, add an elevator, buy new sound and lighting equipment, and build a window-dominated façade. The renovated concert hall now seats 1,995. Smith, founder of Adtran, had come from a musical family.

Propst Arena. Also in 2008, Huntsville businessman William Propst announced a $5 million gift for a major renovation and expansion of the VBC sports arena. It added 1,000 seats (for a total of 9,000), created a large lobby with glass front, added VIP suites and boxes, and improved the over-all concourse. Propst had arrived in Huntsville in 1946 and in the early 1960s set up Propst Drugs in the Five Points area of the city. He had recently sold a drug manufacturing company for a reported $1 billion.

WEEDEN HOUSE MUSEUM. Two years after the Weedens moved to Huntsville in 1832 (see 13. Weeden Mountain), Dr. Weeden died leaving five small children - and a sixth, Maria Howard, arrived six months later. After the Civil War, Mrs.

Weeden divided the property of the estate among her children, and left her home on Gates Avenue to unmarried daughters Howard and Kate.

Maria Howard Weeden painted with water colors, mostly portraits of old ex-slaves and the Negro servants of her neighbors. She also recorded their stories in poems written in Negro dialect. She became nationally known when her books of poetry and paintings were published. There are four: *Shadows on the Wall* (1898), *Bandanna Ballads* (1899), *Songs of the Old South* (1900), and *Old Voices* (1904).

Howard died in 1910, Kate in 1918. The house passed through several owners and was finally sold to the Huntsville Housing Authority in 1976, from which it is leased and operated by the Twickenham Historic Preservation District Association as a museum.

W.T. HUTCHENS BUILDING. This building is on the southwest corner of Jefferson Street and Clinton Avenue. It was built in 1916 and was used by The Hutchens Company for more than 50 years. The W.T. Hutchens name is in stone at the top of the building.

James Madison Hutchens, a carpenter, moved to Huntsville from Tennessee in 1857. He married Lucy Hodges a year later. James served a term on the city council and ran twice, unsuccessfully, for mayor. He and Lucy had six children, one of whom was William Thomas Hutchens, born in 1859. W.T. married Willie Armstrong in 1886, and they had seven children. In 1887 W.T. opened a plumbing and heating business; later it included hardware. He was successful in politics, too, elected to the city council, then for three terms as mayor. W.T. was also U.S. Postmaster in Huntsville appointed by Presidents McKinley, Roosevelt, and Taft, and was active in Republican national politics. His seven children included Morton McAllister, Willard

Coxey, and Vernon Fisher Hutchens. Those three children are the ones whose initials are on the plaque at the Terry-Hutchens Building. W.T. Hutchens died in 1940.

YARBROUGH OFFICE CENTER. This office building at Washington Street and Holmes Avenue opened in 1924 as the Yarbrough Hotel, an 80-room hotel, one of three (the Russel Erskine and Twickenham were the others) that served downtown visitors during the mid-20th-century years when the business of the city was still centrally located. An article in the September 27, 1923, *Huntsville Weekly Times* tells that the hotel was almost ready and mentions its new owners, William and Walter Yarbrough. They were owners of Yarbrough Brothers Hardware, which operated a couple blocks away. The hotel closed in 1968.

9. LIBRARIES

The Huntsville-Madison County Public Library system consists of the big main building at the corner of Monroe Street and St. Clair Avenue plus several branches elsewhere in Huntsville and libraries in other communities. The main building opened in 1986. Branches include ones on Bailey Cove Road, Blue Spring Road, Cavalry Hill, and five that are named for people. Libraries in other communities are those in Gurley, Madison, Monrovia, and Triana.

BESSIE K. RUSSELL BRANCH LIBRARY. Bessie King's great grandfather was one of the county's earliest settlers and tobacco farmers. However, she was born in Huntsville, in 1895. She graduated from Butler School in 1911 and later obtained a degree at Athens College. At 16, she started teaching - up to twelve grades in a one-room school - and continued to teach for several years. She married Dr. C. H. Russell in 1920. In 1947 she took a part-time job with the Huntsville Public Library, where she worked for over 25 years. Ultimately she directed the library's Heritage Room, which houses the large history and genealogical collections. The branch that bears her name, on Sparkman Drive in northwest Huntsville, was established in 1975, when she was 80.

Today (2017) there are plans to re-design or renovate the next-door Public Safety Training Academy, perhaps turning the entire site into a new North Huntsville Library and Community Center.

CAVALRY HILL PUBLIC LIBRARY. Opened in 2017, it is on Poplar Avenue NW to serve the Northwoods Housing community.

ELEANOR E. MURPHY BRANCH LIBRARY. Eleanor Murphy grew up in Athens, Georgia, graduated from the University of Georgia there, then in 1940 obtained her master's degree in library service from Emory University. She worked for the Atlanta Public Library and Georgia Tech library before getting married in 1944. By 1953, she and her family had moved to Huntsville, and she began working for the city's library. She was head librarian from 1958 to 1960, and became an assistant director in 1961. In 1977 she became the library's director, a position she held until she retired four years later. Over-all, she served in the local library system for 28 years. The branch that bears her name is on Charlotte Drive in south Huntsville.

ELIZABETH CARPENTER PUBLIC LIBRARYOF NEW HOPE. In 1992 New Hope's new library, part of a renovated general store built in 1909, was dedicated to Elizabeth Carpenter. She was then 85. Miss Carpenter was born in New Hope, graduated from Huntingdon College in 1928, received a second degree from Peabody College for Teachers in 1931, and during a sabbatical from teaching, got a master's degree from New York University in 1949. Her career began as teacher and librarian at New Hope High School in 1930. She was known as "Miss Library" to hundreds of students and town residents.

JANE GROTE ROBERTS AUDITORIUM. Many people attend activities at the main library in its first-floor auditorium that carries this name. Jane's family was well known in Huntsville: her father was Dr. Carl Grote, her husband Roscoe Roberts. Jane was a leader for 35 years with Friends of the Library and on the HMC Library Board. Jane died in 2007.

MONROVIA LIBRARY. Woody Anderson died in 2003. In April 2004, Congressman Bud Cramer gave the County $100,000 to help build a new Monrovia library to be called The Woody Anderson Library. The name partially stuck: the resulting library today shares two names – Monrovia Library and the Woody Anderson Learning Center.

Anderson grew up in Elkmont. He began dealing in used cars, ran a Plymouth-Dodge dealership from 1950 to 1961, then took over as the Ford dealer and ran Woody Anderson Ford for over 40 years. He was not only a successful businessman, but had statewide connections especially during the Wallace years and was a relatively quiet benefactor behind many local projects.

OSCAR MASON BRANCH LIBRARY. This branch library is part of the Oscar Mason Community Center at Sparkman Homes, part of Huntsville Housing Authorities buildings.

SHOWERS CENTER BRANCH LIBRARY. This branch library is part of the Dr. Richard Showers, Sr., Recreation Center on Blue Spring Road. It's thus also known as the Blue Spring Branch Library.

TILLMAN HILL PUBLIC LIBRARY. The Tillman Denton Hill Public Library in Hazel Green is dedicated to the former Madison County commissioner. Hill had retired from the commission after 20 years, and had long dreamed of and worked toward a library for the community. Much of the money was raised over several years from private sources through Friends of the Tillman Hill Library, then matched by government funds. Hill, suffering from cancer, was present to cut the ribbon when "his" library opened in 1997.

10. HIGH SCHOOLS

ANNIE MERTS CENTER. Annie C. Merts was born in Huntsville in 1881. She taught two years in Madison County (at Green Grove, then Keg's Mill) and 49 years in Huntsville (1923 to 1952). She served as the first president of the Huntsville Teachers Association, and became assistant principal of Huntsville High. Merts died in 1955.

The former Huntsville High School building on Randolph Street (across from her home) has been converted for board of education and related Huntsville school offices and has been named in her honor.

HUNTSVILLE HIGH SCHOOLS. Huntsville operates six high schools, Huntsville High, New Century Technology High, and four that have special names:

Columbia High School. Named to commemorate the loss of the Columbia space shuttle in 2003. The shuttle had successfully gone on 27 missions over 22 years before disintegrating during re-entry near the end of its 28th mission, resulting in the deaths of all seven crew members. The school is located in the southwest portion of Cummings Research Park.

Grissom High School. Virgil Ivan Grissom was born in Indiana in 1926. He graduated from Purdue University in 1950, then served in combat with the Air Force over Korea and as a test pilot, when he was chosen in 1959 in the first group of seven astronauts. "Gus" Grissom piloted Mercury-Redstone 4, the second Mercury suborbital flight, in 1961. He was command pilot for Gemini 3, the first test of the two-man spacecraft (John Young was the other astronaut). He had been selected to be commander of the first Apollo flight in 1967, when during a launch simulation on the pad at Cape Kennedy, a fire broke out in the spacecraft cabin. Grissom, Edward White, and Roger Chaffee were killed before anyone could get the complex hatch open.

Three new Huntsville schools were dedicated to the astronauts in December 1967. They were Grissom High School, Edward H. White Junior High School, and Roger B. Chaffee Elementary School. Astronaut Russell L. Schweickart, a member of the Apollo 9 crew, came to Huntsville for the dedication and represented all astronauts.

Jemison High School. Dr. Mae Jemison was born in nearby Decatur, Alabama, in 1956. She graduated from Stanford, then went to Cornell Medical College. Before she got her medical degree she visited and studied in Cuba, Kenya, and Thailand. After she became a doctor, she set up practice in Los Angeles. A turn as Peace Corps medical officer for Sierra Leone and Liberia came next. In 1985, Jemison made a career change, being accepted into NASA's astronaut training program. As an astronaut in 1992, she flew into space aboard the Endeavor, spent eight days experimenting on the crew and herself. She was the first African American woman to travel in space

Jemison left the astronaut corps in 1993 and is currently a professor at Dartmouth where she has started the Jemison Institute for Advancing Technology in Developing Countries.

Lee High School. Lee High School is "indirectly" named for Robert E. Lee. It reportedly took its name from U.S. 72, "Lee highway," which ran a couple blocks from the original school.

Robert E. Lee was born in Virginia. His father was Revolutionary War hero Henry "Light Horse Harry" Lee and friend of George Washington. Robert graduated from West Point. He married Mary Ann Randolph Custis, great granddaughter of Martha Washington by her first marriage, and for many years lived in Arlington in the Custis mansion, now part of Arlington Cemetery. Lee was commissioned in the Corps of Engineers and held a variety of assignments, including one during the Mexican War with Winfield Scott's force that fought to Mexico City. From 1852 to 1855, Lee was superintendent of West Point. At the start of the Civil War, Lee refused command of Federal forces, instead was loyal to his state and offered his services to the Confederacy. He became its brilliant commander, one of the most famous and respected soldiers in American history, and a symbol of the South. After the war, Lee became president of Washington College, now Washington-Lee University, and devoted himself to education.

MADISON HIGH SCHOOLS. The city of Madison has two high schools with historic names:

Bob Jones High School. The school on Hughes Road is named for Robert E. "Bob" Jones of Scottsboro, who served 30 years (1947-77) in the U.S. Congress from the district that includes Madison County. The school was established in 1974. It moved to its current site in 1996,

James Clemens High School. There were numerous farmer families in the area, but James Clemens is considered the founder of Madison when in 1854 he bought lands halfway between Decatur and Huntsville. This school that bears his name lies south of U.S. 72 on County Line Road. The school opened in 2012. (See 7. In and Around Madison for more about Clemens.)

MADISON COUNTY HIGH SCHOOLS. Three of the county's high schools take their names from the communities they are in: Buckhorn, Hazel Green, and New Hope. Madison County High School is next to Gurley, although it doesn't carry the Gurley name. These four community names were detailed in 2. County Cities and Communities. However, one County school does bear a person's name:

Sparkman High School. The school at Jeff Road and Ford's Chapel Road as well as the community around it is named for Senator John Jackson Sparkman. Sparkman was born in 1899 in Hartselle. He was educated at the University of Alabama, then practiced law in Huntsville until 1936 when he was elected to the U.S. House of Representatives, where he served five terms. There during World War II, he was on the Military Affairs Committee, and helpful to the growth of Redstone Arsenal.

In 1946 when Sparkman had been nominated for a sixth term, long-time Senator John Bankhead, Jr., died, and Sparkman decided to seek that vacant seat. In the general election, his name appeared as the Democratic candidate for both the House and Senate seats. He is probably the only American political figure to be elected to both the House and Senate at the same time and on the same ballot.

In 1952, Sparkman was selected to run for vice president on the unsuccessful Democratic ticket with Illinois Governor Adlai Stevenson. Sparkman served in Congress for over 40 years, until 1979. He died in 1985.

11. COLLEGES AND UNIVERSITIES

Huntsville is fortunate to be home to three universities, a combination community and technical college, and a vocational school. I have made arbitrary decisions in selecting just a few of their named facilities and the leaders, historic figures, and donors involved. Their stories may surprise you.

ALABAMA A&M UNIVERSITY. The school was founded in 1875 as Huntsville Normal School. Part of the original campus is listed on the National Register of Historic Places.

Councill Hall. William Hooper Councill was born a slave in North Carolina in 1848 and was brought to Huntsville by owner Judge D.C. Humphrey. The self-educated Councill was active in the labor movement of the 1870s, a minister and founder of St. John's African Methodist Episcopal Church in Huntsville, editor (1877-1884) of the *Huntsville Herald*, and a successful lawyer (admitted to the bar in 1883). But Councill is best known as the founder of Alabama A&M University. Councill served as its principal from 1875 to 1890 when it was the Huntsville Normal School, and as its president from 1890 to 1909 when it was the State Agricultural and Mechanical College for Negroes and moved to its present location. Councill died in 1909.

A larger-than-life statue of Councill faces Meridian Street on the north side of the campus. It was erected in 2004.

Ernest L. Knight Living and Learning Complex along Meridian Street opened in 2006. It is a huge five-story suite-style dormitory for upper-class students. Dr. Knight graduated from A&M in 1953 and has been one of the school's largest donors.

John & Ella Byrd McCain Health & Counseling Center.
From Meridian Street it is hard to miss this 2014 building
because of the large white letters on its side. John McCain served
as deputy superintendent of Jefferson County schools, and
established an Alabama A&M extension program in
Birmingham. Ella McCain is a graduate of A&M and has served
over 40 years in Jefferson County schools.

Louis Crews Physical Education Complex. The biggest
football field in the area is named for Alabama A&M's
successful football coach, Louis Crews.

Crews was born in Bessemer in 1917, played football and
basketball there at Dunbar High School. He came to Alabama
A&M and lettered three times in basketball and three in football.
He spent four years in the Army during World War II after
which he went to Ohio State for his B.S. degree, later earning an
M.S. from Alcorn State and a P.E. Directorship from Indiana.
In 1960, Crews returned to Alabama A&M as head football
coach. In his first year, his record was 7-1. In 1963, his team
went undefeated, and remained undefeated in conference play for
four years. He took his teams to the Magic City Classic sixteen
times and won it ten - once seven times in a row. He coached
Bulldog teams to several conference championships, produced
several players who went on to become professional players
(John Stallworth is perhaps best known), and won numerous
awards including being named "Outstanding Citizen of
Huntsville." During his coaching career Crews compiled a
record of 110-61-3. Crews died in 2003 at age 87.

L.R.Patton Building. In 1971 the Alabama Legislature named
the school's administration building the L.R. Patton Building.
The name may be old, but the present facility is relatively new.
Leander Patton retired in 1985 after 40 years of service and died
in 1989. (See 8. HHA, L.R. Patton apartments.)

R.D. Morrison Fine Arts Building. Dr. Richard David Morrison was president of Alabama A&M University from 1962 to 1984. A fine arts building – music, art, theatre - on campus has borne his name for decades. He authored two books, one of which is *The History of Alabama A&M University*. Morrison was 103 years old when he died in 2011.

Wilson, McCormick Buildings. In 1911 Virginia McCormick, inventor Cyrus McCormick's daughter, who lived at Kildare in Huntsville, gave a huge donation to Alabama A&M for building a domestic science building and a hospital. In the 1990s, what had been the Virginia McCormick Home Economics Building was renovated and renamed the James Hembray Wilson Building. It is home of the Alabama State Black Archives Research Center and Museum and is open to the public.

James Hembray Wilson was born in Kentucky in 1880. He went through high school in Cincinnati, then graduated from Moody Bible Institute in Chicago. He excelled in music, was considered a master of the cornet, and was a fixture in traveling variety shows. In 1908 he succeeded W. C. Handy as Alabama A&M bandmaster and instructor of vocal music. He eventually held several staff positions culminating as the first black to be named treasurer of Alabama A&M. Wilson retired in 1951 after 43 consecutive years of service.

The building next door to the Wilson Building is now designated McCormick Hall, site for English and foreign languages.

CALHOUN COMMUNITY COLLEGE was founded in Decatur in 1947. Its Huntsville campus is on Wynn Drive, across I-565 from the Space and Rocket Center. The Math-Science-CS building that dominates the campus opened in 2016.

The college is named for John C. Calhoun of South Carolina - orator, states rights advocate, and constitutional lawyer who might have become president if he had not been so uncompromising.

John Caldwell Calhoun was born in South Carolina in 1782. He graduated from Yale University, studied law in Connecticut, returned to South Carolina to practice, and quickly entered politics. In 1810 he was elected to the U.S. House of Representatives, where along with Henry Clay he was a "war hawk," leading to the War of 1812 with England. In 1817 President Monroe made Calhoun Secretary of War. He was vice president under Presidents Adams and Jackson, but after quarrels with the latter, he resigned. Calhoun was then elected to the Senate. President Tyler appointed him Secretary of State, but Calhoun was re-elected to the Senate, where he served until his death in 1850.

FAULKNER UNIVERSITY. Faulkner University is named for Alabama philanthropist James "Jimmy" Herman Faulkner.

James Faulkner was born in Lamar County in 1916. He wanted to be a journalist, so he went to the University of Missouri, where he graduated in 1936. He started his newspaper career in southern Alabama the same year by going into debt and buying the *Baldwin Times*. For years Faulkner claimed he was in debt - at the same time giving away millions of dollars to good causes.

In 1940, Faulkner became mayor of Bay Minette, then in World War II joined the Army Air Corps and became a pilot and flight instructor. After the war, politics beckoned, and Faulkner became state senator and chairman of the Education Committee, where he was the strongest advocate of Alabama's community college system. He unsuccessfully ran for governor in 1954 and 1958. He devoted much of the remainder of his life in business affairs - so successfully that he was once named "Person of the Century" by Bay Minette and Baldwin County.

11. Colleges and Universities

In 1942 the Montgomery Bible School was established. In 1953 the first bachelor degrees were conferred in Bible, and the name was changed to the Alabama Christian College. During the 1970s, the Montgomery campus expanded, and four centers were created elsewhere, including the one in Huntsville that is on Wynn Drive. In 1983, the College name was changed in his honor to Faulkner University. Faulkner died in 2008.

J. F. DRAKE STATE COMMUNITY AND TECHNICAL SCHOOL. In 1947 a legislative act created the Huntsville Vocational School. Land for the school, on Meridian Street, was given by Alabama A&M University. It took until 1962 for facilities to be built and the first students to attend. The school was one of 27 vocational-technical schools created under the "Breakthrough in Education" program of Governor George Wallace. In 1966 the name was changed to honor Dr. Joseph Fanning Drake. In 2013 Drake State was given the full name shown above.

Drake was born in Auburn in 1892. He obtained his B.A. degree from Talladega College and his M.A. from Columbia University. In 1920 he was appointed supervisor of adult education for the Alabama Department of Education. After five years he took over as dean of what is now Alabama State University in Montgomery. In 1927 he became president of Alabama A&M University, a position he held for 35 years until his death in 1962.

S.C. O'Neal Library/Technical Center. This building was the first added to the campus in 23 years when it opened in 2005. It is named for Drake's first president who served from 1962 to 1983.

OAKWOOD UNIVERSITY. Oakwood College was a full four-year liberal arts college, founded in 1896 by the General Conference of Seventh-day Adventists. Back then it was called

Oakwood Industrial School, and according to legend, was named for a stand of oak trees on the campus. In 2007 the college became Oakwood University.

Blake Center houses the administrative offices of Oakwood. It is named for Walter J. Blake, sixth principal (1906-11) of the school.

Burrell Hall. Natelkka Burrell was born in Brooklyn, eventually held a master's degree from Wisconsin and a doctorate from Columbia. She came to Oakwood in 1939 as dean of women where she spent 22 years, implementing a curriculum for teacher education. Over-all she gave 50 years of service to the Seventh-Day Adventist education system. She died in 1990 at age 95.

Cooper Science Complex. Dr. Emerson Cooper graduated from Oakwood in 1948. In 1959 he got his Ph.D. degree in chemistry from Michigan State – the first holder of an Oakwood undergraduate degree to earn a doctoral degree. Dr. Cooper spent 49 years at Oakwood as student, professor, and one time as interim president. The large science complex is named for him.

Cunningham Hall. Eugenia Cartwright was born in 1878, a daughter of former slaves. She grew up in Mississippi, where in 1882 she was caught in the flood when the levee system broke in 700 places. Her schooling was interrupted for jobs to help pay family doctor bills. She was over 35 when she came to Oakwood to complete high school. In 1917 she married Lewey Cunningham. She was employed at Oakwood as superintendent of the orphanage, later matron of the dining room, manager of the school laundry and store, and dean of women – all for over 50 years. She was known to alumni as "Mother Cunningham." The women's residence hall was named for her, but in 2013 it underwent a $5 million renovation to become the student information center.

11. Colleges and Universities

Dred Scott Site. There's a marker on the south side of the Blake Center recognizing Dred Scott. It says "The famed slave Dred Scott lived here on the Peter Blow Plantation from 1819 to 1821 before moving to Missouri, Illinois, and Minnesota. Dred Scott's lawsuit for his freedom helped define one of the many causes of the Civil War." Below is a little longer version of his life.

Scott was born in Virginia about 1799, a slave of the Peter Blow family. He was originally named Sam, but on death of a brother, took his brother's name, Dred. In 1819, Blow bought a quarter section of land where Oakwood University stands and moved to Huntsville - slaves too - to begin a cotton plantation. When the college opened in 1896, its first students were housed in log cabins old enough to have been built by Scott and fellow slaves.

The plantation failed, and in 1821 Blow moved to Florence where he opened the Peter Blow Inn, and later the Jefferson Hotel. In 1830 Blow moved to St. Louis and sold Scott to Dr. John Emerson, a military surgeon. Emerson used Scott as a valet, and as Emerson went on assignment to Illinois and Wisconsin, Scott went along - although slavery was prohibited in those states by the Missouri Compromise. In 1846 Scott filed suit in Missouri for his freedom, having lived so long in those free states. The case went all the way to the U.S. Supreme Court, where in 1857 in the infamous Dred Scott Decision, the court held that a Negro was not a citizen, a slave was property, and the Missouri Compromise was unconstitutional. The decision was one of the events that lead to the Civil War.

In 1857, Mrs. Emerson (Dr. Emerson had died) returned Dred Scott to the Blow family, where he was given his freedom. He didn't get to enjoy it much, as he died the following year.

Eva B. Dykes Library, Archives, and Museum. Eva Beatrice Dykes, a model of academic excellence, was born in Washington, D.C., in 1893. She graduated from Howard

University there, taught English for a year at Walden University in Nashville, then entered Radcliffe College for further study. Radcliffe did not accept Dykes' degree from Howard, so she started over, gaining a B.A. (magna cum laude) in 1917 and an M.A. a year later. In 1920, she joined the Seventh-day Adventist Church. In 1921, she got her Ph.D., one of three black women that year who were the first ever to receive the degree.

Dykes taught for nine years at what is now Dunbar High School in Washington, then joined the Howard faculty for fifteen more. She edited one book, authored another, and wrote many articles - in 1934 for *Message Magazine*, she began a column, and continued it for 50 years. In 1944 she was invited to Oakwood to head the English Department. She was the first faculty member with a Ph.D. She retired in 1968 but was called back in 1970 for another five years - for a total of over 50 years of teaching. In 1978 the new library, archives, and museum building was opened and named for her. Dykes died in 1986 at age 93.

McKee Business and Technology Building. In 1934 at the height of the Depression, O.D. McKee and Anna Ruth McKee paid $200 for a Chattanooga bakery. In the 1950s, the Southern Adventist University invited the McKee Baking Company to their campus. As of 2013, the McKee's Little Debbie products were being sold worldwide – reportedly 900 million cartons of them a year. Through the years the McKee family has shared their philanthropy to include a major gift to Oakwood underwriting the new facility that bears their name.

Peters Media Center was built in 2014 from a $1.2 million gift from Leroy and Lois Peters. The former fine arts building provides an environment where art and today's technology can merge. It also houses the Oakwood Broadcasting Network. The Peters operate a successful home health care business in Maryland.

Peterson Hall. This major building is named for Frank Loris Peterson. In 1917 this teacher accepted an invitation to teach at Oakwood Junior College, as it was then known, and did so until 1925. In 1945 he returned to Oakwood as its president, serving in that capacity until 1954.

UNIVERSITY OF ALABAMA - HUNTSVILLE. The road that winds through the northern side of the campus is Ben Graves Drive, named for the first president of UAH who took office in 1970. He had been president of Millsaps College in Mississippi. The road through the southern part of the campus is John Wright Drive, named for UAH's second president, who succeeded Graves in 1979. Wright had been vice chancellor of West Virginia University.

Bevill Hotel and Conference Center. One of the best-kept secrets at UAH is its hotel, open to the public. Its meeting rooms are used by military and civilian firms, many from nearby Cummings Research Park.

The Bevill Center is named for U.S. Congressman Tom Bevill, who was chairman of the Energy and Water Development Subcommittee of the House Public Works Committee and largely responsible for obtaining the federal funds needed for the building. The facility was originally a learning center for the Corps of Engineers. Bevill was born in Townley, Alabama, in 1921, obtained his B.S. and LL.B. degrees from the University of Alabama, practiced law in Jasper for 18 years, and was elected to Congress in 1966, where he served for 30 years, retiring in 1997. He died in 2005.

D.S. Davidson Invention to Innovation Center. This is a gift from Dorothy Davidson, CEO of Davidson Technologies, for high-tech businesses seeking new starts and for students who will provide new ideas. Construction is underway (early 2018) making this the newest building on campus.

11. Colleges and Universities

M. Louis Salmon Library. Louis Salmon was originally from Mobile, obtained his B.S. and J.D. degrees from University of Alabama, and became a Huntsville lawyer in 1950. In 1962 he was one of the founders of the non-profit group supporting a University of Alabama in Huntsville. In 1986 he became chairman of the Alabama Huntsville Foundation. He worked in many civic, educational, political, and business activities for over 43 years. Salmon died in 1993. Chairman of the Huntsville Madison County Chamber of Commerce said at the time that "There are those people who really make a difference. ... Salmon was one of the people who made Huntsville what it is." The library was named for him in 1996.

Morton Hall. It's where English, arts, humanities, and social studies are taught, and it contains a black box theatre. It's the first and oldest building on the campus.

Morton Hall is named for Dr. John R. Morton who was dean of the Extension Division of the University of Alabama in Tuscaloosa. He was the individual who took the lead in efforts to establish a center in Huntsville. The center, as it was called back then, opened in 1950 and occupied space in a West Huntsville school. This hall - the center's first structure - was opened in 1961 and named for Dr. Morton.

Olin B. King Technology Hall. Olin King was born in Georgia in 1934, hailed from six generations of Methodist ministers, and was expected to follow his father into the ministry. Instead he studied math, physics, and engineering. He arrived in Huntsville in 1957 and helped build the first U.S. satellites while working for ABMA. In 1961 King founded the Huntsville-based company Space Craft Inc., later SCI Systems Inc., with two partners. It grew to have 24,000 employees worldwide and annual revenues over $1 billion.

King Hall was once part (Plant No. 3) of SCI. King was a long-time member of the UA System board of trustees, a supporter and benefactor of UAH, and one of the South's most inventive entrepreneurs. He died in 2012.

Robert "Bud" Cramer Research Hall. The National Space Science and Technology Center was re-named for Cramer in 2004. He was honored for his effort in obtaining funding for the center and for the local home of the National Weather Service housed in the center. Work in the center includes advanced rocket propulsion studies and understanding origin of the universe. The center is across Sparkman Drive from the UAH main campus. You need a security clearance to work there.

Roberts Hall. In 1988, the Humanities Building was named for Dr. Frances Cabaniss Roberts. Dr. Roberts impacted on the many people who have researched and studied local history.

Roberts was born in Gainsville, Alabama, in 1916. At 15 she went to nearby Livingston College, and by 17 she had a certificate and her first teaching job. She used to visit her aunt, Fannie Cabaniss, in Huntsville, and when the aunt died in 1937, Roberts moved to Huntsville to the Cabaniss family home on Randolph Street. She began teaching in Huntsville at West Clinton School. In 1942 she started teaching history at Huntsville High School, which she did for ten years.

Roberts also began efforts to help establish a university extension center (eventually UAH), and served on the committees for its creation, to find the site, and for the first building. She is considered one of the founders of UAH. Roberts then began teaching at UAH in 1950 and taught 25 different courses in history over 30 years, before retiring in 1980. Dr. Roberts died in 2000.

11. Colleges and Universities

Shelbie King Hall. Olin King, head of SCI Systems, supported construction of this building which stands in front of the hall holding his name. It was named for his wife Shelbie King in 2004. It houses UAH's administrative offices, from the president's office to the payroll department.

There is a plaque on the building that describes Shelbie King: "Alumnus, advocate, and supporter of UAH [Shelbie King] displayed a leadership role in enriching the quality of life in the Huntsville community through her philanthropy and work on boards of historic, arts, and music organizations."

Shelby Center for Science and Technology. Richard Shelby is a fifth-generation Alabamian and graduate of the University of Alabama. He served eight years in the Alabama Legislature, then four terms in the U.S. House of Representatives, before being elected to the U.S. Senate in 1986. He was chairman of the Senate Intelligence Committee from 1997 to 2001, and is now Chairman of the Senate Rules Committee and Senate Banking Committee. Shelby also serves on the Senate Appropriations Committee and was responsible for obtaining funds necessary for the building.

The large 207,000-square-foot center is a $60 million facility that contains 18 teaching laboratories, 15 research laboratories, two auditoriums, and almost 150 offices. It was dedicated and named for Senator Shelby in 2007.

Spragins Hall. Marion Beirne Spragins had been president of the Chamber of Commerce in the 1940s. In the 1960s he was given the Huntsville Distinguished Citizen award. Later he was co-founder of the UAH Foundation. In 1973 a gift of 1,000 acres of industrial property was bequeathed by Spragins to the Foundation. He was later memorialized on campus when the UAH gym was named in his honor.

Wilson Hall was built in 1987 and served as the UAH science building. In 1993 it was re-named for the former College of Science dean Harold J. Wilson. Wilson had been a long-time faculty member, beginning as an associate professor in 1972, biology department chairman in 1976, and dean from 1984 to 1991. He died in 1991 after a heart attack at his home. He was only 51. The Wilson Building currently houses a small theatre, art gallery, faculty and student clinics, and is home to Osher Lifelong Living Institute classes for adults.

VIRGINIA COLLEGE. The original Virginia College was founded in 1983 in Roanoke, Virginia – hence the name. In 1989 the college was purchased by Education Futures, Inc. In 1992 Virginia College opened its first branch in Birmingham (now its headquarters are there), and in 1993 opened one in Huntsville (now at 2021 Drake Avenue). It has campus sites in over 25 cities in the southeastern U.S.

The college is run by Education Corporation of America, a for-profit organization. It offers courses such as those in health care, cosmetology, criminal justice, paralegal, and network engineering, plus training in some trades such as truck driving.

12. MOUNTAINS, CREEKS, AND BRIDGES

ALDRIDGE CREEK. According to James Record, in 1811 William Aldridge bought land in the county. Aldridge Creek appeared as early as on an 1817 map (drawn by Huntsvillian F. Sannoner). But by the 1830 census, there was no Aldridge listed in the area.

The creek gained notoriety when it flooded much of southeast Huntsville in the spring of 1999. Today it is the site of Aldridge Creek Greenway, providing five miles for walking and biking along the side of the creek.

BERRY MOUNTAIN. In 2004 Jean and daughter Lynne Berry gave part of Berry Mountain to the Land Trust of Huntsville & North Alabama. The mountain was named for Jean's grandfather, J.T. Berry and his brother Ephraim Jacks Berry who settled in the Maysville area after the Civil War.

B.W. BLAKE MEMORIAL BRIDGE. There are several bridges over Pinhook Creek, but only one named for someone. This one crosses the creek near downtown on Holmes Avenue.

Benjamin William Blake came from Cohn, Ireland, to the United States in 1837. About 1849 he settled in Huntsville near this location. B.W. became street superintendent and served Huntsville in that capacity before and after the Civil War. He also served two terms as city councilman. And he married Sarah Hall. In 1870, the city purchased part of the Blake estate to create Glenwood Cemetery.

Son J.W. Blake became street superintendent too. In the 1800s, J.W. started J.W. Blake Plumbing Company, then he and son Hall C. Blake made it Blake Brothers Plumbing, and finally Hall took over and it became H.C. Blake Company, the name it has today. It was operated, before he retired, by the grand nephew of B.W. Blake, Hall Bryant, who gave me this information.

In 1909 it was J.W. who built the first bridge in this locale over Pinhook Creek. In 1989 the City Council officially named the Holmes Avenue bridge the B.W. Blake Memorial Bridge.

C.B. "BILL" MILLER BRIDGE. The road behind the von Braun Center and Embassy Suites is Heart of Huntsville Drive. (That name comes from a former mall at its location.) Parallel to the street are railroad tracks that serve the Huntsville Madison County Railroad. At the point where the waters from Big Spring Park and Pinhook Creek come together, the railroad crosses over an old-fashioned wooden trestle bridge. The bridge can best be viewed from the Rotary plaza at the west end of Big Spring Park.

The railroad bridge is named for Bill Miller of Miller and Miller, Inc. He erected bridges, drains, buildings and structures for all kinds of agencies across the state and for which he received national recognition. He holds a patent for a culvert forming process for bridge construction. In 2008 the City of Huntsville dedicated and named this little trestle bridge in his honor.

BRIER CREEK is one of the tributaries to the Flint River. *Brier* is apparently the English-preferred spelling of *Briar*, as in the Battle of Brier Creek in Georgia during the Revolutionary War.

CHAPMAN MOUNTAIN. The big hill that highway U.S. 72 crosses in northeast Huntsville is known as Chapman Mountain.

Reuben Chapman moved to Huntsville from Virginia in 1824 and was admitted to the bar a year later. He moved to Morgan County, from which he was elected to Congress in 1835, serving until 1847 when he returned to Huntsville. Right away he was urged to become Governor of Alabama, and he served from 1847 to 1849. During the Civil War, his home was burned, and he was held prisoner by Union troops. Chapman had owned land around the mountain, and in 1873 he bought a home there, where he resided until his death in 1882.

ECHOLS HILL. In downtown Huntsville, Echols Hill is named for Major William Holding Echols, who once owned the LeRoy Pope home atop the hill. (See 4. Echols Avenue.)

FAGAN CREEK. This stream begins at a spring on Monte Sano Mountain, runs down the west side of the mountain through the Blossomwood subdivision, crosses California Street, and follows Lowe Avenue through the city. Huntsville now has most of the creek walled and/or concreted (and wisely so), so it looks more like a drainage ditch than the free-flowing creek it once was. It is named for Peter Fagan, who owned land on the side of the mountain as early as the 1820s, and was the town barber, with his shop on Jefferson Street.

GARTH MOUNTAIN. The hill between Whitesburg Drive and Jones Valley, from U.S. 431 on the north to Weatherly Road on the south, is known as Garth Mountain. It is named for the family that owned the land and the valley east of it from the 1880s to 1940. (See 6. Garth Road.)

GREEN MOUNTAIN. Its color is green much of the year, but that's not how it got its name. It's named for Charles D. Green, a settler on the mountain in the 1800s. According to one write-up, Green was born Kurt Gruene in 1828 in Europe, came to America in 1849, and settled here in the 1860s. According to another, there were claims by a Green as early as 1838. But both agree, whatever his origin, he was a carpenter - cabinet and casket maker. Green died in 1902 and is buried in Maple Hill Cemetery.

HOMER G. "BUDDY" GATLIN MEMORIAL BRIDGE. Gatlin began working for the county's public works department when he was 16. By the time he retired in 2002 after a 57-year career, he had been a part of the paving of almost every road in the county. Gatlin died in 2013. The bridge spans the West Fork of the Flint River on Floyd Hardin Road, a few feet south of Bobo Section Road.

KEEL MOUNTAIN. East of Huntsville's Green Mountain and Hampton Cove, the next large mountain is Keel Mountain. On its east side, near the county line with Jackson County is Keel Mountain Road. Jesse Keel and his wife Priscilla Whitaker were from North Carolina, coming to North Alabama some time before 1819. They settled in what is now Keel Hollow. In 1841 they moved to the mountain itself, and it is named after Jesse. They had 12 children. Jesse died in 1846, Priscilla in 1870.

MADKIN MOUNTAIN. Looking from the east, one can see two prominent mountains on Redstone Arsenal. The one to the left or south is called Madkin Mountain, to the right or north is Weeden Mountain.

I believe Madkin Mountain is a misnomer. The 1909 G.W. Jones map, plus 1906 courthouse records, show the land to be owned by Mrs. Elizabeth Madkin. However, I could find no further information about a Madkin family in Madison County. Then and earlier, adjacent lands were owned by the Matkins family, sometimes written Matkin, even Mattkin. Some of their lands were in the name of Elizabeth G. Matkins. There's even a Matkin Cemetery on Redstone Arsenal with two grave markers, for Elizabeth's daughter Margaret Matkin and granddaughter Mary Patton Matkin. Were these neighboring families with similar names? If not, and they are likely not, shouldn't this be Matkins Mountain?

MONTE SANO MOUNTAIN. In 1827, Dr. Thomas Fearn, along with his brothers Robert and George, established a small community on the big mountain directly east of downtown

Huntsville, near its medicinal springs. Dr. Fearn sent patients to the springs, and some were reportedly cured. He is credited with naming the mountain "Monte Sano," Spanish for "Mountain of Health."

PILL HILL. The hilly area from Governors Drive, south to Drake Avenue, and east of Whitesburg Drive is known as Pill Hill because of the many doctors who have homes there.

PINHOOK CREEK. This is the little stream that runs from Wade Mountain through downtown Huntsville after which it is joined by Big Spring and Fagan Creek waters enroute to the Tennessee. There seems to be no local story as to why it's called Pinhook. Former city hydrologist Warren Campbell said the creek was so named because of its meandering "sinuous" nature.

William Read in an issue of the Louisiana State University *Bulletin* offers the background of a Louisiana Pinhook Bridge. He says the Pinhook word might have come from early settlers' mispronunciation of Indian word "pinsahuck," which stands for the linden or basswood tree.

RAINBOW MOUNTAIN. It's in Madison, and it's a misnomer. (See 7. In and Around Madison.)

RUSSEL HILL. This rise on West Holmes Street is named for Col. Albert Russel who moved to Huntsville in 1816, purchased the hill, and made his residence there. He had served seven years as a Revolutionary War soldier. He died in 1818 and is buried in Maple Hill Cemetery. Descendent Russel Erskine is named for him.

SHARP MOUNTAIN. The mountain, at the far eastern edge of the county, and Sharp's Cove, the valley beneath it, take their names from John Sharp, who arrived here with his wife Martha and ten children in 1809. They were from Pennsylvania, via Kentucky. He had been a major in the Revolutionary War.

WADE MOUNTAIN. The mountain on the north side of Huntsville takes its name from the Wade family. (See 3. Bob Wade Lane and 13. Wade Mountain Nature Preserve.)

WALTON'S MOUNTAIN. Travelers driving over the big hill between Airport Road and Carl T. Jones Drive go over land given by the Fleming family to connect the two. The real estate development atop the hill was created by Walton Fleming, area developer, landowner, and community activist who died in 1996. The Fleming family's home is at the base of the mountain (actually Garth Mountain) on Whitesburg Drive.

WARD MOUNTAIN. At the north tip of the mountains on Redstone Arsenal, near the U.S. Space and Rocket Center, is Ward Mountain, named for George W. Ward, who owned the land in the area as early as the 1860s.

WEEDEN MOUNTAIN. Looking from the east, one can see two prominent mountains on Redstone Arsenal. The one to the left or south is Madkin Mountain, to the right or north is Weeden Mountain. Dr. William Weeden had settled in Marengo County, Alabama. When his wife died, he remarried and, in 1832, moved to Huntsville, where he purchased land on the mountain that now bears his name. (See 8. Weeden House Museum.)

13. PARKS AND RECREATION AREAS

Huntsville has over fifty parks, nine greenways (with another twenty proposed), four huge nature and wildlife preserves, and many recreation facilities. Madison and Madison County add more. Here are over 25 stories of names found in those places.

BERACHAH GYM. The Hebrew name *Berakhah* refers to a traditional blessing or benediction. It was the name of a church academy, and when the city took it over, it kept the name. Today Berachah gym is in back of the Huntsville Public Safety Training Academy (for police and firemen) on Sparkman Drive.

There are plans to re-design the next-door Bessie Russell Library and move or renovate the Training Academy, turning the entire site into a new North Huntsville Library and Community Center.

BIG SPRING PARK. The park features the "big spring" that the Indians knew and at which John Hunt settled. The spring itself provides a flow between 7 and 20 million gallons per day, depending on the time of year. Re-landscaped and expanded in 2017, the surrounding park is a major feature of downtown Huntsville and center for outdoor arts and music events. Madison County Courthouse square is up a bluff to the east, and the von Braun Center is to its west. Ten-story Embassy Suites provides accommodations at the park.

John Q. Hammons Bridge. Monroe Street passes through the park and over the canal formed by the big spring. In 2006 Mayor Loretta Spencer named that bridge over the canal for Hammons. It was his company that made the investment in the resulting Embassy Suites Hotel. There are dedication plaques on the bridge, visible from below.

Rotary Plaza. Built in 2010 to honor Rotary Club members, it's where the water leaves the park.

Tom Thrasher Fountain. Between Embassy Suites and the von Braun Civic Center is a little plaza with benches, a circular basin, and large fountain. In 2005 the Thrasher family donated the fountain and setting in memory of their father, Tom Goodman Thrasher. On an adjacent stone monument and plaque his many civic accomplishments are listed, such as – just to pick three - being president of the Huntsville Industrial Expansion Committee, director of the Huntsville-Madison County Chamber of Commerce, and chairman of the von Braun Civic Center and Visitors Bureau Board.

BILLY HUNTER PARK. About 40 years ago, Billy Hunter let softball players play ball on some acres he owned north of Hazel Green. In 1979 he helped build the town's first real ball field. Hunter, whose business was Tall Pines Construction Company, was an ardent sports fan. About 1992 the county bought 20 acres beside Hunter's property. Hazel Green Athletic Association then bought 40 more acres of Hunter's land. Now there are several baseball, football, and soccer fields plus a gym for basketball. All of this was known as Hazel Green Park, but in 2002 the park was renamed for Hunter. Hunter had died the year before.

BRAHAN SPRING PARK. By 1811, land in Madison County was so popular that the federal land office was moved from Nashville to Huntsville. Prices rose from the original $2 per acre to hundreds, even thousands of dollars per acre. In 1818 there was another great land sale. John Coffee, the surveyor general of the local land office, joined with Andrew Jackson and other Nashvilleans to bid on and buy up the choicest land. But they met stiff opposition, much from John Brahan, the receiver of public money at Huntsville. Brahan was able to buy over 40,000 acres. Unfortunately, he did this with government money, and when public funds were needed, he came up thousands of dollars short. He was investigated by a congressional committee but pleaded he did it to save local land from wealthy speculators, and was convincing enough that he wasn't prosecuted. It is some of that land and its spring and lake that now bear his name.

The park is a few blocks west of Memorial Parkway on both sides of Drake Avenue. Toward the south is the $22 million Huntsville Aquatics Center that opened in 2017. Toward the north are kids playgrounds, picnic shelters, and football stadium. The park also contains a disc golf course; it was the first in Alabama.

Milton Frank Stadium. Milton Frank, originally from Nashville, starred on the football team at the University of Tennessee. Immediately after graduating in 1934, he came to Huntsville as teacher and football coach at Huntsville High School. He held those positions for twelve years. In 1946 Coach Frank, as he was known, left to become co-owner of Rose Jewelry Company; he was also vice-president of a jewelry business in Mobile. The change gave Frank time to be active in civic affairs. He became president of the Shriners and the Optimist Club, board member of Christmas Charities and the Huntsville Industrial Expansion Committee, and for five years a director of the Boys Club - to name a few. Coach Frank died in 1967 at age 56. A few weeks before his death, the state legislature voted to change the name of Huntsville Stadium to Milton Frank Stadium.

CAPT. TREY WILBOURN MODEL AIRPLANE PARK. Down Leeman Ferry Road toward the city's solid waste disposal area is the entrance to a field for flying kites and remote controlled airplanes. The field is home to the Rocket City Radio Controllers. Huntsvillian Wilbourn, for whom it is named, was a 28-year-old Marine Corps pilot killed in 1991 during Operation Desert Storm when his jet was shot down over Iraq.

CAVALRY HILL. This park on Poplar Avenue is part of the Cavalry Hill Academy for Academics and Arts magnet school. The Buffalo Soldiers Memorial stands in front of it.

Following the Spanish-American War, as many as 14,000 veterans were in Huntsville. The U.S. Surgeon-General declared Monte Sano one of the two healthiest places in the nation (West Point was first), and veterans with yellow fever were sent there to recuperate, while others tried to avoid the disease that was sweeping the Gulf Coast. One of the soldiers' lasting efforts was the building of the fountain, the one seen today at the start of the Big Spring.

CREEKWOOD PARK. It is a couple blocks east of Slaughter Road and connects to the Indian Creek greenway. There's green space, a kids play area, and a disc golf course.

DR. RICHARD SHOWERS, SR., RECREATION CENTER. The Blue Spring Recreation Center was rebuilt in 1995 and has expanded several times since then. It houses gym facilities, swimming pool, and branch library. There are ball fields behind it. The center was named for city councilman Dr. Richard Showers, Sr. Showers graduated from Alabama A&M University with B.S. and M.S. degrees, and holds an honorary doctorate. He was elected to the Huntsville city council in 1988, representing the north district of Huntsville, and held that position until 2016. He served on numerous planning commissions and boards over his long tenure on the council.

FERN BELL. This sports complex (baseball and soccer fields, tennis courts, gym, and basketball facility) west of Whitesburg Drive at Sanders Road is named for Fern Bell, president of the Huntsville American (youth baseball) League 1967 to 1969.

GOLDSMITH-SCHIFFMAN WILDLIFE SANTUARY. Margaret Anne Goldsmith and her family donated the land to the city for this 375-acre sanctuary. A hiking trail goes through pristine bottomland forest, wetlands, and springs near the Flint River. An observation point displays the name JoBaLa, for Goldsmith's three children, John, Barbara, and Laurie. In the Hampton Cove area, the sanctuary can be accessed on its south end from Taylor Road just south of Terry Drake Road.

June and AJ Brannum Parking Area. The Sanctuary can also be accessed at its north end from U.S. 431 via an unmarked unpaved road just south of Hampton Cove Storage Units. At the end of the road is a parking area donated by June and A.J. Brannum. A.J. was a well-known home builder from nearby Big Cove. From the parking area, a hiking trail, partially paved, leads into the sanctuary.

HALSEY FAMILY PARK. At the corner of California and White Streets, there's a little park. Although there's no sign, it commemorates the family of the Halsey Grocery business. (See 8. Halsey Grocery.)

HAYS NATURE PRESERVE. This preserve of over 500 acres was part of about 4,000 acres that Dr. Burritt inherited in the 1800s. Burritt left the land to a trust, and the Hays family bought the land from the trust in 1986. They asked ecologist Susan Weber to develop a plan for the area, and in 1999 the family donated the preserve to the city with the stipulation it be named for J.D. and Annie S. Hays. It consists of land virtually untouched for more than a hundred years - teaming with wildlife and displaying spectacular trees. The preserve, entered from U.S. 431 just south of Hampton Cove, opened to the public in 2002. There is a small information center, two roads, and several trails. The Flint River Greenway and the Big Cove Creek Greenway trails intersect with the preserve.

JAMES C. CRAWFORD PARK. Crawford played sports at Alabama A&M winning nine varsity letters. After graduating, he began officiating and was the first black member of the Alabama High School Athletic Association, a membership he held for 45 years. This park, just south of the A&M campus, was named for him in 2001.

JOHN HUNT PARK. The park is named for the man who settled at the big spring in 1805, but it shouldn't be confused with Big Spring Park. It is the name given to the 400-plus acres that used to be the old airport. It stretches south along Leeman Ferry Road from Joe Davis Stadium on the north, across Airport Road, past the **Huntsville Tennis Center**, to the **Huntsville Cross Country Running Park**. It includes what used to be the Becky Peirce Golf Course.

Benton H. Wilcoxon Ice Complex. Benton Hartung Wilcoxon was a native of California, but he and his wife were residents of Huntsville for 50 years. He helped develop Randolph School and served on its board of directors. More importantly, Wilcoxon was an avid skier, liked winter sports, and was the major figure in bringing ice sports to this part of the South. He opened The Ice Palace on Governor's Drive in 1958, giving the city its first ice skating rink. He was a founder of the Ice Skating Institute (ISI) of America, and in 1995, he was named to its Hall of Fame. He was involved in the original proposal for the building on Leeman Ferry Road that bears his name. Wilcoxon died in 1997.

Joe Davis Stadium. Joe W. Davis was elected mayor of Huntsville five times, serving for twenty years, from 1968 to 1988. One way to look at the length of his tenure is to realize that, when he took office, America had not gone to the moon; when he left office, the Apollo program was old history. During his years as mayor, Huntsville never had a budget deficit, and its credit rating was upgraded. His administration oversaw construction of the Von Braun Center, the Huntsville Madison County library, and Interstate 565. But one of his favorite projects was for a stadium and a minor-league baseball team.

When the stadium was constructed in record time so that the Huntsville Stars could begin play, the city council named the stadium after him. Davis died in 1992 at age 74.

The Huntsville Stars left Huntsville in 2014 to become the Biloxi Shuckers. At this writing (2017) the stadium stands empty and is used only for occasional events. Some plans call for it to become an amphitheater.

Mincher Road. Entrance to the stadium from Memorial Parkway is on Mincher Road, named for the president of the Southern (baseball) League, Don Mincher. Mincher was born in Huntsville in 1938, made it to the major leagues in 1960, played thirteen seasons (with Washington, Minnesota, California, and Oakland), was named to the 1967 and 1969 All-Star games, and played in the 1965 and 1972 World Series (winning with Oakland in the latter).

JONES FARM PARK (aka Jones Family Park) provides walking space around an attractive pond between Four Mile Post Road and Carl T. Jones Drive.

KEN JOHNSTON PARK. In 1991, Buelah Johnston Huggins gave ten acres near Mountain Gap and Bailey Cove Roads to the city for a park to be named for her husband, Ken Johnston, who had been a prominent Huntsvillian for many years.

KENT ROBERTSON PARK. Kent Robertson was active in recreational activities in his neighborhood, playing T-ball and baseball and spending time in the park. When he tragically died in 1988 at the age of nine, neighborhood friends got the city to change the name of Logan Park, on Logan Drive in southwest Huntsville, to Kent Robertson Park.

LAKEWOOD PARK is officially on York Road, but it is a block north of Mastin Lake Road on Kenwood Drive. It contains the Lakewood Community Center and ball fields, one of which is named John Steigerwald Field. John had been a coach in the northern part of the city for several sports, including baseball.

MADISON COUNTY NATURE TRAIL. Madison County operates two parks, Sharon Johnson Park and this one located atop Green Mountain. There is a large pond with a trail around it and a pavilion with hillside picnic tables.

MCGUCKEN PARK. William V. McGucken began working for the Huntsville Parks and Recreation Department in 1974. He became chairman of the American League (youth baseball) board of directors, helped organize the city's youth soccer program, and assisted the city in acquiring park properties in south Huntsville. McGucken died in 1983. The park that now bears his name is on Bailey Cove Road south of Hobbs Road.

MERRIMACK PARK is on Triana Boulevard where Merrimack Mill once stood. The City has converted it to accommodate ten soccer fields.

MONTE SANO NATURE PRESERVE. On Monte Sano Mountain, this preserve covers over 1,100 acres and is one of the largest urban preserves in the country. There are over 25 miles of hiking and biking trails. The preserve is managed in partnership with the Land Trust of North Alabama.

SHARON JOHNSTON PARK. This park halfway between Buckhorn and New Market is named for Sharon Ann Johnston Leithoff. She was a stunt pilot, killed in 1974 when her single-engine biplane crashed during an air show in Massachusetts. In 1978, her family donated over 250 acres of land for the park in her honor. The park includes camping sites, swimming pool, track, ball fields, shooting range, picnic areas, and a small lake. The lake is named **Jimmy Johnston Lake** after her father.

13. Parks and Recreation Areas

STONER PARK. On Bragg Street that runs between Mastin Lake and Stringfield Roads, this relatively large park has ball fields, tennis courts, and kids play equipment. It is named for Henry Stoner, builder of homes on Huntsville's north side. He designed the park and constructed its main ball field back in the 1960s.

WADE MOUNTAIN NATURE PRESERVE. Atop the mountain that is north of Huntsville (see 3. Bob Wade Lane), Land Trust of North Alabama has created an 843-acre Nature Preserve. Over eight miles of trails have been developed. There are also two waterfalls and six springs, one of which forms the headwaters of Huntsville's Pinhook Creek.

WELLMAN FAMILY PARK. In 1915, Willard I. Wellman and his wife Helen gave the little triangular area (one of the "points" at Five Points) between Pratt and Holmes Avenues to the city for use as a park. It took until 2002 for the park to be landscaped and finally officially named Wellman Family Park. The sign needed to identify it is being redone.

14. REDSTONE ARSENAL

There are over 70 military and civilian organizations on Redstone Arsenal, and unless you are a military person, many of their names are confusing. Rather than agency and commanding officer names, this chapter tells stories behind the names of Arsenal facilities and roads – those places that survive passing history, at least for a while.

A BRIEF REDSTONE ARSENAL HISTORY. In 1941 the U.S. Army was authorized to construct a chemical manufacturing and storage facility to augment the one the Chemical Warfare Service (CWS) had at Edgewater, Maryland. An area of over 7,700 acres southwest of Huntsville was selected, and named Huntsville Arsenal. About the same time, the Army's Ordnance Department needed new facilities for ammunition production. Recognizing the economy of locating next to the new CWS installation, the Chief of Ordnance acquired 4,000 adjacent acres. During the World War II years that would follow, Arsenal personnel produced a variety of munitions including incendiary and smoke devices, gas bombs, and demolition blocks.

In 1941 Majors Carroll D. Hudson and H. Sachs made several trips to Huntsville, and one of Major Sachs' assignments was to recommend names for Ordnance plants. According to Hudson, he, Hudson, wanted the name Redstone because of the red rock and soil in northern Alabama. Major Sachs agreed. And, as Colonel Hudson has written, "no one else objected" so the name Redstone became official.

As infrastructure for the Arsenal was created, many of the names of its roads and buildings stem from this and earlier eras.

14. Redstone Arsenal

After WWII the Chemical Corps declared Redstone surplus to its needs. At the same time, the Ordnance Corps needed more space for its new rocketry and missile responsibilities. In 1949 Ordnance took over the Huntsville Arsenal area, facilities, and operation of all of Redstone Arsenal. That same year, the group of German rocket scientists who had surrendered to the U.S. at the end of WWII and had been located at Fort Bliss, Texas, were authorized to be re-located to Redstone Arsenal and Huntsville to continue their work on rockets.

During the 1950s the Army developed the Redstone and Jupiter missiles and made possible the country's first satellite, Explorer I. In 1960 a big change occurred when all nonmilitary space-oriented missions were re-organized under the National Aeronautics and Space Administration (NASA). Such activities were transferred from the Army Ballistic Missile Agency to the new Marshall Space Flight Center (MSFC). That center was headquartered on the Arsenal where it remains today. MSFC is credited with placing the first American in space, developing the Gemini and Apollo programs, and creating the Saturn rockets that enabled man to visit the moon in 1969.

ARMY AIRFORCE MEMORIALS. In the 1940s an airstrip was built to accommodate planes used to test various chemical bombs and grenades. A simulated wooden village was built as one of the targets. Over the years, planes dropped more than eight million pounds of chemical munitions onto Huntsville Arsenal.

On June 27, 1944, a fully loaded B-26 Martin Marauder took off but developed engine trouble. The plane caught fire and crashed in a cotton field just north of U.S. 72 and about nine miles from Huntsville. The bombs exploded.

Hale Road, which connects the airstrip with Rideout Road, is named for 1st Lieutenant Emmett J. Hale, the pilot. He had been among the first group of Army Airforce officers stationed at Redstone in 1943.

Loeffler Park is named for 2nd Lieutenant Jerome Loeffler, the bombardier.

Valim Reservoir, the Arsenal's water reservoir on Madkin Mountain, is named for Sergeant Antone Valim, the flight engineer.

BUILDINGS. When Huntsville Arsenal was first created, over 500 families had to move. More than 500 buildings, three schools, and 14 churches were lost, some among the oldest structures in Madison County. Today, many of Redstone Arsenal's buildings are known only by numbers. Here are some of the few, however, that have been named for people.

Col. Stephen K. Scott Fitness Center. The Family and Morale Welfare and Recreation directorate has made four fitness facilities available at the Arsenal. One is the Scott Center on Digney Road. Col. Scott was the highest ranking officer killed in Operation Iraq Freedom (i.e., the Iraq war) when he was killed in the Baghdad Green Zone in 2008. Col. Scott was from nearby New Market.

Fox Army Health Center. Except for the commissary, perhaps the building most visited by retired military is the hospital. The Fox Army Hospital officially opened in 1978. It was named for Brigadier General Leon Alexander Fox (1891-1965), a Birmingham native whose career as an Army doctor spanned more than 30 years. He served in two world wars and earned 16 medals and decorations, including awards from the British and Italian governments.

Harris Home. This home of the Harris family was built by Sam Harris, Sr., in the 1920s, reportedly around an existing log cabin from the early 1800s. From the 1800s, the Harris family owned and farmed 1,000 acres here that stretched south to the Tennessee River, and they lived in the home until the Army bought it in 1941. At that time Sam Harris, Jr., bought the Bob Wade property north of Huntsville. (See 3. Bob Wade Lane.) The Harris home still stands on Buxton Road, a lone reminder of life in the area before Redstone Arsenal.

John J. Sparkman Center, Heflin Buildings, and Bob Jones Auditorium. When it opened, the Sparkman Center was the largest building project on Redstone Arsenal. The Center is a campus-style complex of buildings that provides facilities for over 3,000 people. The first six buildings opened in 1994, and the complex was dedicated to Senator Sparkman. (See 10. Sparkman High School.)

In 1998 two more buildings were added and called the Heflin Buildings for Alabama Senator Howell Heflin. Heflin graduated from Birmingham-Southern College and the University of Alabama Law School. He was elected as chief justice of the Alabama Supreme Court, then in 1978 to the U.S. Senate. He retired in 1997. Heflin was a supporter of Huntsville and Redstone Arsenal endeavors, especially area missile research and development and construction of nearby I-565.

The auditorium at the Sparkman Center has been named for former Congressman Bob Jones. (See 10. Bob Jones High School.)

McMorrow Missile Laboratories. Major General Francis McMorrow was a West Point graduate with an Ordnance career that spanned over thirty years. In 1962 he became the first commanding general of the U.S. Army Missile Command. Just after his death in 1963, the Arsenal's then-new missile research and development facility was named for him.

Shelby Center. The Missile & Space Intelligence Center has been named for Senator Richard C. Shelby. Shelby served on the Senate Armed Services Intelligence Committee and was largely responsible for authorizing and obtaining funds for the building. (See 11. Shelby Center for Science and Technology.)

Von Braun Complex. Adjacent to the Sparkman Center, this much larger set of buildings (simply called von Braun 1, 2, 3, and 4) mainly houses the U.S. Army Space and Missile Defense Command. The facility opened in 2011. (See Section 8, Von Braun Center.)

BUROSE ROAD. Missile Command Headquarters are on this road. It once connected the NASA and Army sectors. It was named for Walter Burose, a popular German scientist in the Structures & Mechanical Laboratory of the Army Ballistic Missile Agency (ABMA) who died in 1956 of a heart attack while out selling brooms for the Lions Club.

HUNTSVILLE ARSENAL CWS ROADS. In 1941 the laying of new roads was one of the first construction projects in preparing the Arsenal. The Chemical Warfare Service memorialized some of its World War I fallen soldiers by naming roads after them. The following were all members of the First Gas Regiment and were killed in France in 1918.

Buxton Road is the extension of Green Cove Road through Gate 2 at the southern part of the Arsenal. It is named for Corporal Vernon C. Buxton, killed in action in the Verdun Sector.

Goss Road is the extension of Drake Avenue, through Gate 8, west to Rideout Road. It is named for 1st Lieutenant Paul L. Goss, who died of wounds.

Martin Road crosses the entire Arsenal, from Whitesburg Drive west through Gate 1, then through Gate 7 nearly to Wall Triana

Road. It is named for Private Herbert B. Martin, killed in action at St. Thibaut.

Neal Road connects Patton and Rideout Roads in the center of the Arsenal. It is named for Private William K. Neal, killed in action at Cite St. Pierre.

Patton Road extends north through the main portion of the Arsenal, through Gate 10, until it becomes Jordan Lane. It is named for Sergeant Gerald S. Patton, who died of wounds. (But there's a different story in 6. Patton Road.)

Rideout Road also extends north through the main portion of the Arsenal, through Gate 9, where it becomes Research Boulevard.. It is named for 1st Lieutenant Percy E. Rideout, killed in action at Verdun. He was posthumously awarded the Distinguished Service Cross.

MARSHALL SPACE FLIGHT CENTER. The Center that honors Marshall's name was activated in 1960 with the transfer of property and personnel from the Ordnance Corps' Army Ballistic Missile Agency. Dr. Wernher von Braun became its director.

In 1961 MSFC's Mercury-Redstone boosted Alan B. Shepard, America's first astronaut, into space. In the 1960s, MSFC developed the Saturn series of rockets that served the Apollo program and eventually lifted man to the moon, then placed Skylab into orbit. MSFC also managed, for examples, the High-Energy Astronomy Observatory series that included the Hubble Space Telescope, the Space Shuttle propulsion systems, and Spacelab.

MSFC is named for General George C. Marshall. Marshall was a graduate of Virginia Military Institute, directed the St. Mihiel and Meuse-Argonne offensives in World War I, served as aide to

General Pershing, and became Army Chief of Staff in 1939, a position he held throughout World War II. In 1947, President Truman named him Secretary of State. Part of the Truman Doctrine was the Marshall Plan, for reconstruction of Europe, for which Marshall received the Nobel Peace Prize in 1953. In 1950, during the Korean War, he was made Secretary of Defense, and became the only person ever to serve as both Secretary of State (1947-49) and of Defense (1950-51). This widely admired officer and diplomat died in 1959.

ORDNANCE ROADS. Several Redstone Arsenal roads, all called drives, are named for Ordnance leaders. They are all short roads off Goss Road in the main post area near the officer and NCO family housing areas. They include:

Bomford Drive. Named for Col. George Bomford, chief of Ordnance 1832 to 1848.

Buffington Drive. Named for Adelbert R. Buffington, chief of Ordnance 1899 to 1901.

Ripley Drive. Named for James W. Ripley, chief of Ordnance 1861 to 1863.

Roberts Drive. The drive is a misspelling. It is supposed to be named for Brigadier General Samuel McRoberts, Ordnance officer with the AEF in World War I and then chief of the New York Ordnance District from 1932 to 1941.

Vincent Drive. Named for Brigadier General Thomas K. Vincent, the first commanding general at Redstone Arsenal, June 1952.

TOFTOY THRUWAY. At the end of World War II, Col. Holger N. Toftoy was chief of the technical intelligence team for the Army Ordnance Corps. It was to his organization that the

German scientists from Peenemunde, the German rocket base, surrendered. In 1945 Toftoy personally flew to Washington to get permission to bring the scientists to the United States, eventually to Huntsville. He was assigned to Washington and given responsibility for the direction of the Army missile program. In 1952 Toftoy was assigned to Redstone Arsenal, as Director of the Ordnance Missile Laboratories, then was promoted to major general and in 1954 became Commander of Redstone Arsenal.

Products created during his command are now historic: Nike Ajax, Nike Hercules, Hawk, LaCrosse, Honest John, Corporal, Redstone, Sergeant, Pershing, Jupiter, Jupiter C, Explorer, and Pioneer.

Toftoy retired in 1960, died in 1967. He is buried in Arlington National Cemetery.

ZIERDT ROAD. Colonel John G. Zierdt was born in 1913, graduated from West Point, and served during World War II in Panama and Europe. From 1956 to 1962, Zierdt had six assignments at Redstone Arsenal, and in 1963 became Commanding General of the Army's Missile Command (MICOM). He served in that capacity until 1967. Zierdt's awards were many and included the Bronze Star. He died in 2000.

15. MORE PLACES OF INTEREST

ALABAMA CONSTITUTION VILLAGE MUSEUM. Its site on Gates Avenue is where the original constitution for the state was written. In May 1819 elections were held for delegates to a constitutional convention. The 44 elected delegates met here in June. John Williams Walker of Madison County was chosen president of the convention, but most of the work to draft the constitution was delegated to a Committee of Fifteen under Huntsville attorney Clement Comer Clay. In August the convention adopted the resulting constitution and adjourned. The constitution was considered ratified and operational so in September general elections were held for state offices and for the general assembly. In October the general assembly met in Huntsville, the state's new capital. In November William Wyatt Bibb, who had been governor of the Alabama Territory from 1817 to 1819, took the oath of office as the state's first governor. Finally, it was on December 14 that President James Monroe signed a congressional resolution that admitted Alabama as the 22nd state of the United States.

The Alabama constitution was put together by some powerful people. Out of the 44 delegates there emerged six governors, six judges of the supreme court, and six U.S. senators.

The Constitution Village Museum consists of several structures that represent years 1805 to 1819. One is the Clay building that housed Clay's office. Another is the Boardman building that contained the printing plant where John Boardman, editor-publisher of the *Alabama Republican* newspaper, printed the first copies of the constitution. A third building is the home of Stephen Neal, sheriff of Madison County from 1808 to 1822. There's also a blacksmith shop and early post office. And Constitution Hall in which all the delegates met.

BUFFALO SOLDIERS MEMORIAL. In 1866, African-Americans were organized into segregated Army regiments that served primarily in the west. The Buffalo Soldiers name refers specifically to mounted regiments of the 9th and 10th Cavalries. During the Spanish-American War, the Buffalo Soldiers served alongside Teddy Roosevelt and his Rough Riders. After the war, the 10th Cavalry was ordered to Huntsville and in 1898-99 camped on the site now known as Cavalry Hill.

In 1996 Dr. John Cashin, whose grandfather had written a history of the Buffalo Soldiers, conceived the memorial. It is a 10-foot high, 35,000-pound black marble base topped by a bronze statue of 10th Cavalry Sgt. George Berry riding his horse up Cuba's San Juan Hill and waving the regimental flag. Mobile sculptor Casey Downing created the statue. The entire monument was unveiled in its present position in 2010.

BURRITT MUSEUM. William Henry Burritt was born in Huntsville in 1869. His father, Dr. Amatus Robbins Burritt, who had a practice in Huntsville for over twenty years, was a pioneer of homeopathic medicine. Son William graduated from Vanderbilt University in 1890, did post graduate work in Cincinnati and New York, returned to Huntsville in 1898, and listed himself as a homeopathic physician.

In 1892 he had married Pearl Johnson, but Pearl had died in 1898 of appendicitis. In 1899 he married Mrs. Josephine Drummond, a wealthy widow from St. Louis. The couple moved there, where Burritt became involved with rubber manufacturing, eventually obtaining patents for improvements to tires. In 1933, Josephine died, and Burritt inherited the bulk of her estate.

Burritt returned to Huntsville, purchased land called "Roundtop" on Monte Sano Mountain, and constructed a unique home. It was insulated with bales of wheat straw - and in 1939, it burned. In the rebuilding, straw was again used, but inside one-inch-thick plaster, and with asbestos siding on the outside. It was odd, but temperature stays between 55 and 80 degrees, and acoustics are excellent. In 1949 Burritt donated his father's home on Eustis Street to the city. In 1955 Burritt died and left his Monte Sano home and property to the city to be maintained as a museum.

CUMMINGS RESEARCH PARK. This is one of the country's leading science and technology parks, covering 3,800 acres, housing 23 of the top 26 U.S. government contractors, home to 300 companies, and employing 30,000 people.

Milton Kyser Cummings was born in Gadsden. As a boy he suffered osteomyelitis and had one leg amputated just below the knee. Much of his life was spent showing others how to be successful despite a handicap.

A Huntsville cotton merchant befriended Cummings, gave him money to go into business. Cummings became a successful cotton merchant, then got out of the business and invested heavily in the stock market - again successfully. In 1958 he took over presidency of faltering Brown Engineering Company and, with much of his own money, built it into the largest machine shop in the South serving the space program. (The original Brown Engineering Company was named for area industrialist Rufus P. Brown.) In 1960, for new buildings, he bought 150 acres - 80 for Brown, the remainder to be sold to other companies at cost. The location would become the initial part of the park that now bears his name.

In addition to his role at Brown, Cummings was involved in local and national campaigns involving health, education, and employment. He was once state senator, served on the school board, and in 1965 was named Huntsville's "Man of the Year."

A research institute and park were ideas of Dr. Wernher von Braun. He believed an industrial park should be developed for companies that would serve R&D requirements of the Army Missile Command and the Marshall Space Flight Center.

It was just after Cummings' death at age 61 in 1972 that the park was named Cummings Research Park.

There are streets within the park named for people, plus this one that's a bit unusual:

Genome Way. This boulevard leads to the HudsonAlpha Institute for Biotechnology and is landscaped in the form of a double helix.

Jan Davis Drive is named for American astronaut Nancy Jan Davis, veteran of three space flights who logged over 600 hours in space. (See 4. Davis Circle.)

Mark C. Smith Drive is named for the founder and CEO of Adtran, a leading provider of networking and communications equipment worldwide. (See 8. Von Braun Center.)

Moquin Drive is named for Brown vice-president Joe Moquin. Cummings bought the original 150 acres, but it was Moquin in 1960 who was assigned the task of finding the place. He went on to be CEO of Teledyne Brown and in the 1980s convinced the city council to expand the park into what is today its 2,000-acre western portion.

DOWNTOWN RESCUE MISSION. DRM began to serve the homeless in 1975. It offers not only temporary housing and meals, but a Christian program for those who want to break their homeless or drug-related lifestyle. In 2008 DRM moved from its original Ninth Avenue location to a new campus on the former Westminster Christian Academy grounds on Evangel Drive. None of its newly acquired buildings have names, except one:

Owens House, shelter for women and children. It is now (2017) under construction. The Owens name was given as a memorial by an undisclosed donor.

FIVE POINTS HISTORIC DISTRICT. In 1999 the City created the Five Points Historic District. Its dwellings (over 35 of them) range from Victorian homes, bungalows from the 1920s and 1930s, some Cape Cod houses, and ranch style homes from the 1950s and 1960s. The District has grown to be bordered by O'Shaughnessy Avenue on the North, Grayson Street on the east, Wells and Eustis Avenues on the south, and Russell Street and Andrew Jackson Way on the west.

GOLDSMITH-SCHIFFMAN FIELD. On Ward Avenue in the northeast part of the city, this athletic field opened in 1954 and was the site of the city's first night game. The land had been donated to Huntsville by Oscar, son Lawrence, and Annie Goldsmith, and Robert and wife Elsie Schiffman, in memory of their wives and mothers. It was donated specifically for use as an athletic field.

Oscar Goldsmith was born in New York City in 1849. A job as a jewelry salesman took him through Huntsville, where he met and married Betty Bernstein. Here he set up a dry goods and clothing store, and later the Goldsmith Grocery Company. He helped get Dallas Mill to the city, was one of its major stock holders, and served as its treasurer. Oscar was also president of the Huntsville Land Company, one of the organizations that led to development of East Huntsville and the present Five Points area. He died in 1937.

Solomon and Daniel Schiffman came to the United States in 1857, Solomon to Cincinnati and Daniel to Paris, Kentucky. They moved to Huntsville before the Civil War and opened a dry goods and clothing business on the courthouse square. Isaac Schiffman, born in 1856 in Germany, came to Huntsville in 1875 to join his uncles, Solomon and Daniel. He married Bettie Herstein; their children were Robert, Irma, and Annie. In 1908 son Robert, by then grown, and son-in-law Lawrence Goldsmith joined the business, which had expanded into cotton and land leasing. Isaac died in 1910. That year, the business incorporated as I. Schiffman & Company. It still operates today at its courthouse square location. (See 8. I. Schiffman Building.)

HARRIS HOME FOR CHILDREN. George Ernest Harris and his wife Chessie Walker Harris moved to Huntsville from Cleveland, Ohio, in 1950. George was grounds superintendent and farm manager, and Chessie was food service director, at Oakwood College. One by one they found homeless, neglected, or abandoned children and provided necessary foster care. In 1954 they founded the Harris Home for Children. George sold the family farm in Ohio to fund the home. The home cared for about 40 children at any one time; during their lifetimes, the Harrises cared for over 900 children. George died in 1988, Chessie in 1997. The home that bears their name continues today as a privately owned foster-care and child placement agency for the Huntsville area and the state of Alabama.

HUNTSVILLE BOTANICAL GARDEN is a 112-acre public garden that originated in 1979 as a garden society with 14 members. The Garden today is governed by a 32-member board of directors and a 30-member advisory council, claims over 2,600 active members, and welcomes about 350,000 visitors a year. There is also a foundation responsible for continuing finances and endowment. Donors are actively sought and dedication names for plants, places, and structures abound. Here are some named facilities visitors might find:

Eloise MacDonald Propst Guest House, result of her major gift to the Garden, provides the Garden's main entrance. The $12 million 3,500-square-foot structure includes rental areas, meeting rooms, café, and gift shop.

John and Tine Purdy Butterfly House is one of the best known Garden facilities. It encompasses 9,000 square feet, lush vegetation, a waterfall, ponds, and streams, and is home to frogs and turtles as well as thousands of butterflies. John Purdy, long-time member still active on the foundation board, is president of Laughlin Funeral Home.

Linda J. Smith Center. It was dedicated in 2005 by late Adtran executive Mark C. Smith in recognition of his wife's love for the Garden. She also remains active on the foundation board of the Garden today.

Murray Hall is a popular site for meetings and parties. It is named for Gary Murray, county extension agent and first president of the originating garden society in 1980.

HUNTSVILLE MADISON COUNTY ATHLETIC HALL OF FAME. It isn't a building, it's a memorial monument of sorts. It stands a few yards west of Memorial Parkway on Johnson Road. The large monument is full of the names of politicians who apparently voted for it. Annual AHOL inductees each have a named brick in the ground aside it.

Vaughn Stewart is credited with the idea. Stewart was from Anniston. At 165 pounds he was the smallest center to play for the University of Alabama. In the 1940s he was selected as a center by the Chicago Cardinals of the NFL, later traded to the Brooklyn Dodgers. He became co-chairman of the first HMCAHOF in 1989 and was himself inducted in 1990. He died in Huntsville in 1992.

J.E. "ED" MITCHELL, JR., INTERMODAL CENTER. Next to Huntsville International Airport on Wall Triana Road is this huge facility, idea of Ed Mitchell, to merge air cargo, rail, and highway operations and to serve the nearby Jetplex Industrial Park. Mitchell was the first chairman of the Airport

---

Authority's board of directors from 1956 to 1968. From 1971 to 1987 he was executive director of the Port of Huntsville during which Huntsville received Port of Entry designation for foreign trade by U.S. Customs. He also aided in land acquisition for Jetplex and for the area of I-565 that serves the airport. The center was named for him in 2007.

OLD TOWN HISTORIC DISTRICT. This District was designated by the city of Huntsville in 1974 and was added to the National Register of Historic Places in 1978. It encompasses over 200 buildings dating from 1828 with most originating from between 1870 and 1930. It is the only predominantly Victorian neighborhood in the city. The District is bounded by Walker Avenue to the north, Dement and California Streets on the east, Wells and Clinton Avenues on the south, and Lincoln Street on the west.

SANDRA MOON COMMUNITY COMPLEX. In 2017 Grissom High School moved to its current location on Haysland Road and left its old location on Bailey Cove Road for redevelopment, which is already underway. The auditorium remains, operated by Arts Huntsville. The gym and recreation fields also remain, operated by the Huntsville Parks and Recreation Department. The main anchor to the site will be a new library.

The entire complex bears Sandra Moon's name. She represented southeast Huntsville on the City Council from 1998 to 2010. She is said to have voted 20,000 times during that tenure. One of her major efforts was to obtain the new library for the area. She talked about it the week she died, in 2013.

THORNTON RESEARCH PARK. In 1983, the University of Alabama Huntsville Foundation bought over 400 acres of Southern Railway property between Highway 20 and Madison Pike. The park is separate from Cummings Research Park although it is adjacent to it. It is named for Vance Thornton, who was in the Huntsville banking, insurance, and real estate business for many years. At time of his death in 1965, he was vice president of the UAH Foundation.

TWICKENHAM. In 1809, LeRoy Pope, the richest man in the county with the most land, bought Hunt's Spring (the name of the settlement before it was Huntsville) and the land surrounding it. He got friends in the Mississippi Territory legislature to rename the community Twickenham and to make it the seat of Madison County. Twickenham was the home of English poet Alexander Pope, a distant ancestor of LeRoy.

But settlers didn't like the name - some were jealous of Pope, others were mad at England with the War of 1812 beginning. So in 1811 local citizens were able to get the legislature to change the name again - to the present one that honors original settler John Hunt.

TWICKENHAM HISTORIC DISTRICT. This District was designated by the City of Huntsville in 1972 and added to the National Register of Historical Places a year later. The District contains over 100 buildings and is one of the largest concentrations of ante-bellum homes in the South - more than 65 such buildings dating from as early as 1814. The District is bounded by Randolph Avenue on the north, White and California Streets on the east, Lowe Avenue on the south, and Franklin Street on the west.

WATERCRESS PONDS. In the years before Huntsville became the Rocket City it was known as the Watercress Capital of the World. Does anyone today still grow and harvest watercress locally? Answer is yes – B&W Growers, a half mile east of New Market on Old Mountain Fork Road.

WHEELER NATIONAL WILDLIFE REFUGE. This refuge stretches along both sides of the Tennessee River in Limestone, Morgan, and Madison counties, mostly between Decatur and Huntsville. It was established in 1938 and covers 34,000 acres.

The refuge is named for General "Fighting Joe" Wheeler. A West Point graduate, but commanding Confederate forces in the Civil War, Wheeler was in 500 skirmishes and commanded 127 full-scale battles. After the war, Wheeler served as U.S. Representative from Alabama in 1881 to 1882, in 1883, and from 1885 to 1900. At age 62, he volunteered at the outbreak of the Spanish-American War and became the only Confederate general to gain that rank again in the U.S. Army as he led a cavalry unit in Cuba. As if that weren't enough, he served further in the Philippines insurrection of 1899 and 1900. Wheeler died in 1906.

WILLIAMS WELL. Huntsville Utilities supplies water to approximately 90,000 families. Surface water is pumped from the Tennessee River and processed through the South Parkway and Southwest Huntsville Treatment Plants. Other water comes from wells that access limestone aquifers and is supplied through the Lincoln and Dallas Well and Hampton Cove Well Treatment Plants, and the Williams Well. That last is located west of the city, and is named for James Williams, land owner in that area.

BIBLIOGRAPHY

Over 50 references were listed in my 2003 version of this book. I have not repeated them here. Instead, with a couple exceptions, I've listed source materials mainly for new entries in this edition.

Allen, Linda Bayer, *Who Was Bob Wallace? A Historical Inquiry,* 2014. Article is available via the Huntsville History Collection web site.

Benson, Reggie, "A&M Legend Crews dies at 87," *The Huntsville Times,* January 21, 2005

Berry, Lucy, "Downtown 'gateway' named for Alabama civil rights icon," *The Huntsville Times,* September 16, 2016

"Celebrating the Life of Doctor Leander Raphel Patton," First Missionary Baptist Church, Huntsville, document, June 20, 1989

Chapman, Elizabeth Humes, *Changing Huntsville, 1890-1899,* Huntsville Historic Foundation, Huntsville, 1989

ci.madison.al.us – Madison, AL – Official Website

Clines, Keith, "Highway will honor fallen public servants," *The Huntsville Times,* May 14, 2010

Connor, Kristen, "Plans moving forward for the former Grissom High ...," for *WHNT 19 News,* July 17, 2017

Districts – City of Huntsville web site

Doyle, Steve, "Maysville family donates property to Land Trust," *The Huntsville Times,* January 17, 2008

Bibliography

Doyle, Steve, "Huntsville's old Lincoln Mill textile factory getting new life," *The Huntsville Times*, September 29, 2009

Doyle, Steve, "Buffalo Soldier memorial rises …," *The Huntsville Times*, November 12, 2009

Doyle, Steve, "Cecil Ashburn … dead at 92," *The Huntsville Times*, July 22, 2012

Doyle, Steve, "… Sandra Moon dies …," for *Al.com*, April 9, 2013

Easterling, Bill, "In Tribute to a Family of Pioneers," regarding the Blake family, *The Huntsville Times*, July 28, 1989

Gattis, Paul, "UAH invention center to influence future," *The Huntsville Times*, October 18, 2017

Gilbreath, Doris B., *Lily Flagg*, Gilbreath Publications, Huntsville, 2001 (p. 60)

Gipson, Laura L., "Port of Huntsville Announces Dedication of J.E. Mitchell, Jr., International Intermodal Center Building," for *hsvairport.org*, May 8, 2007

Harbarger, Harvilee Phillips, "The Huntsville Madison County Botanical Garden 1979-1997," *Huntsville Historical Review*, Summer-Fall 1997

Haskins, Shelly, "Dr. Julian Davidson … Dies," *AL.com*, February 1, 2013

http://blacksdahistory.org for Burrell, Cunningham, Peters biographies

http://www.notablebiographies.com/Ho-Jo/Jemison-Mae, html

Bibliography

http://www.wow.com/wiki/Fox_Henderson

https:/en.wikipedia.org/wiki/Jan_Davis
https:/en.wikipedia.org/wiki/George_Clinton_(vice_president)
https:/en.wikipedia.org/wiki/Lowe_Mill
https:/en.wikipedia.org/wiki/Mark_C_Smith
https:/en.wikipedia.org/wiki/Maysville
https:/en.wikipedia.org/wiki/Space_Shuttle_Columbia
https:/en.wikipedia.org/wiki/Vaughn_Stewart
https:/en.wikipedia.org/wiki/Virginia_College

https://www.huntsvilleal.gov/meet-huntsvilles-premier-architect-2/ for the biography of George Steele

Huntsville Botanical Garden, Celebrating 25 [years], 1988-2013, Craftsman Printing, Inc., 2013

Huggins, Paul, "Bridge named for Madison County worker," regarding Homer Gatlin, *The Huntsville Times*, February 14, 2014.

Huggins, Paul, "Paul Luther Bolden Memorial Highway ...," on Twitter, August 21, 2013

Jeffcoat-Trant Funeral Home, Opelika, AL, Obituary: Brent Allen Wheeler, September 19, 2012

Kesner, Kenneth, "Librarian just can't keep quiet," re S.C. O'Neal library, *The Huntsville Times*, September 26, 2005

Lawson, Brian, "Vann Pruitt led Huntsville crime lab ...," http://blog.al.com, January 21, 2012

"Looks like Pinhook is here to stay," Ask Us column, *The Huntsville Times*, May 1, 2005

Bibliography

Marshall, Mike, "Alleys aid 'sense' of community," *The Huntsville Times*, September 3, 2010

Marshall, Mike, "There goes the neighborhood" (about Pension Row), *The Huntsville Times*, February 27, 2007

Marshall, Mike, "Living Legend" (W.L. Halsey), *The Huntsville Times*, October 1, 2006

Marshall, Mike, "In downtown Lick Skillett, Ala. ...," *The Huntsville Times*, December 21, 2010

Marshall, Mike, "At Harris Home, 'we treat them as family'," *The Huntsville Times*, December 19, 2010

Marshall, Mike, "BRAC Circle is a symbol of growth in Huntsville's real estate market," *The Huntsville Times*, September 4, 2011

Middleton, Karen, "Seaboard Abandons Track to City," *The Huntsville Times*, November 9, 1983. Much of the L&N story came from Bob Baudendistel, local railroad historian

"Mr. Leander R. Patton" biography, from Alabama A&M Archives, Mildred L. Stiger, Archivist

NationalCAC.org for Children's Advocacy Center information

O'Brien, John, "If You Burn It, They Will Come: The Housing Authority in Huntsville, 1941-1960," *Huntsville Historical Review*, Fall 2013

Peck, John, "VBC Makeover starts in spring," *The Huntsville Times*, December 18, 2008

Perszyk, Judy, "Five Points, Our Streets and Avenues," Five

Bibliography

Points Historical Association *Newsletter*, 2015

Rankin, John P., *Memories of Madison*, The Donning Company Publishers, Virginia Beach, Virginia, 2007

Reeves, Wendy, "911 Center named after Potts," *The Huntsville Times*, April 9, 2009

Roberts, Janet, "Guard armory gets a name", *Huntsville News*, April 16, 1980

Ropp, Lee, "VBC plans $15M arena facelift and expansion," *The Huntsville Times*, October 24, 2008

Shiver, Joshua, "Huntsville Botanical Garden," *Encyclopedia of Alabama*, December 2, 2016

Slaten, Julie, "Alabama Constitution Village," *Encyclopedia of Alabama*, February 22, 2017

Slaten, Julie, "Huntsville Depot and Museum," *Encyclopedia of Alabama*, March 2, 2017

Spires, Shelby G, "Cramer Hall Honors Bud's Perseverance," *The Huntsville Times*, September 28 2004

Tuscaloosanews.com, "Joseph C. Dowdle," posted August 22, 2004

United States Department of Justice website for Levi Lincoln information

Ward, Michael D., *Shaping History – The University of Alabama Huntsville Foundation*, Author House, Bloomington, IN, 2008

Whiteaker, Larry, "Battle of Dug Hill," *Herald-Citizen*, Cookeville, TN, March 7, 2010

INDEX

A Brief Redstone Arsenal, History, 128
Adams Street, 30
Airport Road, 48
Alabama, 7
Alabama A&M University, 100
Alabama Constitution Village Museum, 136
Alan B. Shepard Highway, 48
Albert Hall Highway, 20
Aldridge Creek, 113
Andrew Jackson Way, 41
Annie Merts Center, 96
Ardmore Highway, 20
Army Airforce Memorials, 129
Bailey Cove Road, 48
Balch Road, 67
Bankhead Parkway, 48
Bannister Alley, 30
Beirne Avenue, 41
Bell Factory, 10
Belk-Hudson Lofts, 71
Benton H. Wilcoxon Ice Complex, 124
Berachah Gym, 119
Berry Mountain, 113
Bessie H. Russell Branch Library, 93

Bevill Hotel and Conference Center, 108
Bevins Gap Road, 49
Bide-A-Wee Drive, 49
Big Spring Park, 119
Billy Hunter Park, 120
Blackwell Medical Tower, 80
Blake Bottom Road, 20
Blake Center, 105
Blount Hospitality House, 71
Blue Springs Road, 50
Bobo, 10
Bob Jones Auditorium, 131
Bob Jones High School, 98
Bob Wade Lane, 20
Bob Wallace Avenue, 50
Bomford Drive, 134
BRAC Circle, 51
Brahan Spring Park, 120
Brier Creek, 114
Browns Ferry Road, 21
Buckhorn, 11
Buffalo Soldiers Memorial, 137
Buffington Drive, 134
Buildings, 71
Burose Road, 132
Burrell Hall, 105
Burritt Museum, 137

Buxton Road, 132
Butler Terrace, 77
Buttermilk Alley, 67
B.W. Blake Memorial
    Bridge, 113
Byrd Spring Road, 51
Calhoun Community
    College, 102
California Street, 52
Capshaw Road, 21
Capt. Trey Wilbourn Model
    Airplane Park, 121
Carl T. Jones Drive, 52
Cavalry Hill, 122
Cavalry Hill Public Library,
    93
C.B. "Bill" Miller Memorial
    Bridge 114
Cecil Ashburn Drive, 53
Cecil Fain Drive, 53
C. F. Post Building, 71
Chapman Mountain, 114
Charles H. Stone
    Agricultural Center, 71
Chase, 11
Church Street, 31
Clinton Avenue, 31
Clopton Street, 53
Cluttsville, 11
Coleman Street, 42
Colleges and Universities,
    100
Col. Stephen K. Scott
    Fitness Center, 130
Columbia High School, 96
Cook Avenue, 54

Cooper Science Complex,
    105
Councill Hall, 100
Countess Road, 21
County Cities and
    Communities, 10
Creekwood Park, 122
Criner Road, 54
Cummings Research Park,
    138
Cunningham Hall, 105
Cruse Alley, 31
Dallas Street, 42
Dan, 12
Dan Tibbs Road, 22
Davidson Center for Space
    Exploration, 88
Davidson Center for the
    Arts, 82
Davis Circle, 31
Deposit, 12
Ditto Landing, 12
Dowdle Center, 81
Downtown Huntsville
    Streets, 30
Downtown Rescue Mission,
    139
Drake Avenue, 54
Dred Scott Site, 106
Dr. Joseph L. Lowery
    Boulevard, 58
Dr. Richard Showers, Sr.,
    Recreation Center, 122
D.S. Davidson Invention to
    Innovation Center, 108
Dublin Park, 68

Dug Hill Road, 22
Echols Avenue, 32
Echols Hill, 115
Elbert H. Parsons Law
   Library, 72
Eleanor L. Murphy Branch
   Library, 94
Elizabeth Carpenter Public
   Library of New Hope, 94
Eloise MacDonald Propst
   Guest House, 141
Elon, 13
England Street, 43
Ernest L. Knight Living and
   Learning Complex, 100
Eunice's Country Kitchen,
   77
Eustis Avenue, 32
Eva B.Dykes Library,
   Archives, and Museum,
   106
Fagan Creek, 115
Fannings Crossing, 13
Farley, 13
Faulkner University, 103
Fearn Street, 55
Fern Bell, 122
Figures Alley, 55
Fisk, 13
Five Points Historical
   District, 140
Floyd E. "Tut" Fann State
   Veterans Home, 72
Floyd Hardin Lane, 22
Ford's Chapel Road, 23

Forensic Sciences Building,
   73
Fort Jackson M. Balch, 74
Four Mile Post Road, 55
Fox Army Health Center,
   130
Franklin Street, 33
Gallatin Street, 33
Garth Mountain, 115
Garth Road, 56
Gates Avenue, 34
Genome Way, 139
Glenn Hearn Parkway, 57
Goldsmith-Schiffman Field,
   140
Goldsmith-Schiffman
   Wildlife Sanctuary, 122
Gooch Lane, 68
Goss Road, 132
Governors Drive, 56
Grayson Street, 43
Greene Street, 34
Green Mountain, 115
Grimwood Road, 23
Grissom High School, 96
Gurley, 14
Hale Road, 129
Halsey Avenue, 43
Halsey Grocery, 74
Halsey Park, 123
Hampton Cove, 14
Harbinville, 14
Harold H. Potts Center, 75
Harris Home, 130
Harris Home for Children,
   141

Harrison Brothers Hardware Store, 74
Harvest, 15
Harvie Jones Building, 75
Hays Nature Preserve, 123
Hazel Green, 15
Heflin Buildings, 131
Henderson National Bank, 76
Heroes Highway, 23
High Schools, 96
Historic Huntsville Depot, 76
Hobbs Island, 15
Hobbs Island Road, 57
Hobbs Road, 57
Holmes Avenue, 34
Homer C. "Buddy" Gatlin Memorial Bridge, 115
Houston Goodson Way, 57
Hughes Road, 68
Humes Avenue, 44
Huntsville, 8
Huntsville Arsenal CWS Roads, 132
Huntsville Botanical Garden, 141
Huntsville Cross Country Running Park, 124
Huntsville High Schools, 96
Huntsville Hospital, 80
Huntsville Housing Authority Buildings, 77
Huntsville Madison County Athletic Hall of Fame, 142
Huntsville Museum of Art, 81
Huntsville Tennis Center, 124
In and Around Madison, 66
I. Schiffman Building, 82
James C. Crawford Park, 123
James Clemens High School, 98
James Record Road, 57
Jan Davis Drive, 139
Jane Grote Roberts Auditorium, 94
Jeff, 15
Jefferson Street, 34
Jemison High School, 97
J.E. "Ed" Mitchell, Jr., Intermodal Center, 142
J.F. Drake State Community & Technical School, 104
Jimmy Johnston Lake, 126
Jim Whitaker Highway, 24
Joe Davis Stadium, 124
Joe Quick Road, 24
John & Ella Byrd McCain Health and Counseling Center, 101
John and Tine Purdy Butterfly House, 142
John Hunt Park, 124
John J. Sparkman Center, 131
John Q. Hammonds Bridge, 119
Johnson Towers, 78

Index

Jones FamilyPark, 125
Jordan Lane, 57
June and AJ Brannum
  Parking Area, 123
Keel Mountain, 116
Ken Johnston Park, 125
Kent Robertson Park, 125
Lacy Street, 44
Lakewood Park, 125
L&N Drive, 58
Lee High School, 97
Leeman Ferry Road, 59
Lewis Crews Physical
  Education Complex, 101
Libraries, 93
Lick Skillet, 16
Lily Flagg Road, 59
Lincoln Mill Office
  Campus, 82
Lincoln Park, 78
Lincoln Street, 35
Linda J. Smith Center, 142
Loeffler Park, 130
Lombardo Building, 83
Lowe Avenue, 36
Lowe Mill, 83
L.R. Patton Apartments, 78
L.R. Patton Building, 101
Madison, 16
Madison County, 7
Madison County High
  Schools, 98
Madison County Nature
  Trail, 126
Madison High Schools, 98
Madison Street, 36

Madkin Mountain, 116
Mark C. Smith Concert
  Hall, 90
Marshall Space Flight
  Center, 133
Marsheutz Avenue, 60
Martin Road, 132
Martin Luther King, Jr.,
  Highway, 25
Mason Furniture Building,
  83
Mastin Lake Road, 60
Max Luther Drive, 60
Maysville, 16
McClung Avenue, 37
McCullough Avenue, 44
McGucken Park, 126
McKee Business and
  Technology Building, 107
McKinley Avenue, 44
McMorrow Missile
  Laboratories, 131
Medaris Drive, 61
Memorial Parkway, 62
Meridian Street, 62
Meridianville, 16
Merrimack Hall, 84
Milton Frank Stadium, 121
Mincher Road, 125
Minor Street, 45
M. Louis Salmon Library,
  109
Monroe Street, 37
Monrovia, 16
Monrovia Library, 94
Monte Sano Mountain, 116

Index

Monte Sano Nature
Preserve, 126
Moontown, 16
Moores Mill, 17
Moores Mill Road, 25
Moquin Drive, 139
More Huntsville Streets, 48
Morton Hall, 109
Mountains, Creeks, and
Bridges, 113
Murray Hall, 142
Nance Road, 69
Neal Alley, 38
Neal Road, 133
Nebo, 17
New Hope, 17
New Market, 17
Nick Davis Road, 26
Oakwood University, 104
Old Railroad Bed Road, 26
Old Town Historic District,
143
Olin B. King Technology
Hall, 109
Opp Reynolds Road, 26
Ordnance Roads, 134
Oscar Mason Community
Center, 79
Oscar Mason Branch
Library, 95
O'Shaughnessy Avenue, 45
Owens Crossroads, 18
Owens House, 140
Palmer Road, 69
Parks and Recreation Areas,
119

Patton Road, 62, 133
Paul Bolden Military,
Museum, 89
Paul Luther Bolden
Memorial Highway, 27
Pension Row, 69
Peters Media Center, 107
Peterson Hall, 108
Pill Hill, 117
Pinhook Creek, 117
Plevna, 18
Pratt Avenue, 46
Propst Arena, 90
Providence, 18
Pulaski Pike, 63
Rainbow Mountain, 69, 117
Randolph Street/Avenue, 38
R.D. Morrison Fine Arts
Building, 102
Ready Section Road, 27
Redstone Arsenal, 128
Rideout Road, 133
Ripley Drive, 134
Rison Avenue, 46
Roads in the County, 20
Robert "Bud" Cramer, Jr.,
National Children's
Advocacy Center, 85
Robert "Bud" Cramer
Research Hall, 110
Roberts Drive, 134
Roberts Hall, 110
Rotary Plaza,120
Russel Erskine Apartments,
85
Russel Hill, 117

Russell Street, 46
Ryland, 18
S.C. O'Neal Library/
Technical Center, 104
Sandra Moon Community
Complex, 143
Searcy Homes, 79
Sharon Johnston Park, 126
Sharp Mountain, 117
Shelbie King Hall, 111
Shelby Center, 132
Shelby Center for Science
and Technology, 111
Showers Center Branch
Library, 95
S.H. Kress Building, 86
Slaughter Road, 70
Sparkman Drive, 63
Sparkman High School, 99
Sparkman Homes, 79
Spragins Hall, 111
Spragins Street, 38
St. Clair Avenue, 63
Steele Street, 64
Steger Road, 28
Stoner Park, 127
Streets in Huntsville's Five
Points District, 40
Stevens Avenue, 47
Sullivan Street, 70
Swancott, 18
Terry-Hutchens Building,
87
Thomas W. Davidson
Senior Center, 87

Thornton Research Park,
143
Tillman Hill Public
Library, 95
Todd Towers. 80
Toftoy Thruway, 134
Tom Thrasher Fountain,
120
Toney, 19
The Beginning of Madison
County and Huntsville, 7
Times Building, 88
Triana, 19
Twickenham, 144
Twickenham Historical
District, 144
University of Alabama –
Huntsville, 108
U.S. Rocket and Space
Center, 88
U.S. Veterans Memorial
Museum, 88
Valim Reservoir, 130
Vincent Drive, 134
Virginia College, 112
Von Braun Center, 89
Von Braun Complex, 132
Wade Mountain, 118
Wall-Triana Highway, 28
Walton's Mountain, 118
Ward Avenue, 47
Ward Mountain, 118
Ward Mountain Nature
Preserve,127
Washington Street, 39

Watercress Ponds, 144
Weatherly Road, 64
Weeden House Museum, 90
Weeden Mountain, 118
Wellman Family Park, 127
Wellman Avenue, 47
Wells Avenue, 47
Wells Road, 28
Wheeler National Wildlife
  Refuge, 145
Whitesburg Drive, 64
Williams Street, 39

Williams Well, 145
Willis Von Moore
  Highway, 29
Wilson Hall, 112
Wilson, McCormick
  Buildings, 102
Winchester Road, 29
W.T. Hutchens Building, 91
Wynn Drive, 65
Yarbrough Office Center,
  92
Zierdt Road, 135

Made in the USA
Middletown, DE
25 August 2024

59150163R00088